The Family Treasury of Antiques

The Family Treasury of Antiques

by
William C. Ketchum, Jr.

A Ridge Press Book

A & W Publishers, Inc.,
New York

Editor-in-Chief: Jerry Mason
Editor: Adolph Suehsdorf
Art Director: Albert Squillace
Project Art Director: Harry Brocke
Associate Editor: Ronne Peltzman
Associate Editor: Joan Fisher
Art Associate: Nancy Mack
Art Associate: Liney Li
Art Production: Doris Mullane
Picture Editor: Marion Geisinger

First published in the United States of America in 1978
by A & W Publishers, Inc., 95 Madison Avenue, New York, New York 10016,
by arrangement with The Ridge Press, Inc.

Library of Congress Catalog Card Number: 78-56890
ISBN 0-89479-033-1

Printed in the Netherlands by Smeets Offset, Weert.

Cover Credits

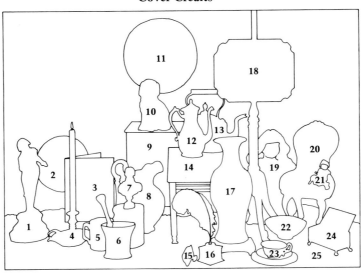

Contents

Introduction
8

Introduction

During the last two decades a veritable revolution has occurred in the antiques field. Not too long ago antiques collecting was almost exclusively the domain of a few very wealthy individuals in a small number of countries. The objects these people collected and regarded worthy of the name "antique" were themselves rather limited. Fine academic painting and sculpture, high-style furniture, gold, silver, and bronze—all dating to the eighteenth century or earlier—were seen as the only true antiques.

All this has changed greatly. Early in the twentieth century artists initiated the change when they became interested in the artifacts of less materially advanced cultures. These pieces, known generally as primitive art (though they were often far from primitive in design and execution), provided a source of inspiration for some of the most important art work of this century. However, because of its limited availability, primitive art has never been widely collected.

Following the Second World War a much larger group of collectors and a wider variety of collectible objects entered the field. Middle- and working-class people, particularly in the United States and western Europe, found themselves with more leisure time and more money than they had ever had before. For many of them, a good deal of this time and money went into the collecting of antiques.

The development of this vast new army of collectors has had profound effects on the antiques field. First, there were not enough items in the traditional categories to meet the burgeoning demand, so the concept of what an antique was began to change. Traditional age barriers toppled. The nineteenth century became "antique," and Victoriana was a new source of inspiration. Even the traditional customs-law definition of anything less than a century old as nonantique was breached. Collectors simply referred to, their new finds as "collectibles" and proceeded to acquire them, even when they had been made only a few decades earlier.

Moreover, the categories of antique objects grew. To sterling silver were added Sheffield and nineteenth- and early-twentieth-century electroplate. Academic painting was expanded to include hundreds of obscure artists whose work had theretofore not been thought worthy of collection. And, following in the footsteps of those who had first acquired primitive art, the new collectors sought out the works of nonacademic artists like sign painters, silhouette cutters, and even amateurs. These efforts became known

German or Flemish bronze aquamanile, 15th century.

as folk art, a category that commands high prices today. Provincial or "country" furniture was welcomed as an adjunct to the scarce and expensive finer traditional pieces. And whole new categories of collectibles appeared—toys, woodenware and basketry, vehicles, advertising materials—dozens of different fields that had never before been regarded as having any merit as antiques.

Finally, as collectors became more sophisticated and well traveled, antiques collecting became international. American basket collectors wanted not only the Indian baskets of their own Southwest, but also French field baskets and woven storage containers from Africa and China. European textile collectors added American quilts to their own nation's tapestries and printed fabrics. It has therefore become necessary for serious collectors to know not only about the antiques of their own areas, but also about those of other lands.

It is in response to this need that this book has been written. It is designed to provide European and American collectors with an informative, illustrated guide to the most popular general categories of antiques and collectibles available throughout the world. The text is written in recognition of the fact that most of the traditional antiques categories are greatly changed from what they were even thirty years ago, and that as more collectors enter the field, more changes will occur. Thus, for example, primitive painting and sculpture, folk art, and fine or academic art, rather than being seen as separate categories, are now treated by many collectors simply as antique art.

This work is designed to offer the average collector an insight into the types of objects he or she may reasonably expect to see and hope to buy. True, certain pieces, such as Chinese bronzes, are likely to be beyond the reach of all but a very few readers. However, it is important that the very early and very rare items be mentioned in order that their relationship to later, more available antiques may be understood.

Many valuable pieces are still waiting to be discovered. They show up almost every day, sometimes in unlikely places, and their discoverers are often informed dealers or collectors. But it is not the author's intention that this book serve as a treasure hunter's guide. For the great majority of collectors, the "treasure" provided by antiques is the satisfaction of finding, studying, and living with the artifacts of the past. If this book can help the reader find that satisfaction, its purpose will have been achieved.

1
Folk Art

Preceding pp.: Primitive American landscape painting, oil on board, *c.* 1825. Paintings of this type were common from the early 19th century until the Civil War. Above: Mexican carved stone sculpture of a laughing face, Vera Cruz, *c.* 1400. This fragment of a larger figure exemplifies sophistication of pre-Columbian sculpture.

For many years, the collecting of painting and sculpture has been an important avocation throughout the world. Chinese emperors of the Sung dynasty (960–1279) collected the works of their court-appointed artists. The ruling princes of the Italian city-states collected the bronze sculpture and oil paintings of the great Renaissance masters. So valued are these works of art that some have been preserved for centuries. Today many are priceless or nearly so and are the exclusive possessions of museums and wealthy collectors.

Such painting and sculpture is generally called "fine art" or "academic art," the latter term referring to the fact that those who created it were systematically trained in the rules of their craft (painters, for example, were taught perspective, color mixing, and line drawing; sculptors were taught anatomy) within a hierarchical system based on a master artist who instructed a number of students. This art had clearly defined styles, and most academic artists adhered to these styles throughout their careers.

Fine art seldom had much to do with the lives of average people. It was supported by the wealthy, and most of it went into their homes or was donated by them to public institutions such as churches. Workers and peasants had little if any contact with fine art. But they did have art of their own.

In the late nineteenth and early twentieth centuries, collectors of more modest means (many of whom were artists themselves) began to discover other types of art. They examined the creations of nonacademically trained craftsmen such as sign painters, figurehead carvers, and woodblock-print makers. They sought out and purchased the strange and powerful sculptures and the delicate gold or bronze miniatures of the so-called primitive societies. Such work did not fit orthodox conceptions of fine art, though often the artist was the product of a tradition as

long and a training process as rigorous as any undergone in the schools of Europe.

Many different names have been applied to such painting and sculpture: primitive art, naïve art, nonacademic art. However, "folk art" has gradually come to be the preferred term, reflecting the fact that most of this work was done by and for the common people and, unlike academic art, which until recently was the exclusive domain of the rich and high-born, was available to them as part of their daily lives. Many definitions of folk art have been put forth, and there is considerable disagreement as to what distinguishes it from academic art. For the purposes of this book, it seems most productive simply to talk about the generally recognized characteristics of the field.

First, folk art may be said to include painting and sculpture in traditional styles, associated with specific communities. For example, when a Maori craftsman in New Zealand carved a house-post figure he worked in a certain manner to achieve a result that would be instantly recognized by the entire community. His figure was not identical to all those made in the past. Rather, it conformed to certain rules of carving and coloring that were customary in the community. Such reverence for time-honored methods of work and modes of decoration is at the heart of all folk art. No matter how fresh and spontaneous, how "accidental," a piece may appear to us, it is far from that to its creator.

Central to such tradition is the concept of the folk artist as a skilled craftsman. Indeed, there are few serious collectors today who still conceive of the folk artist as a simple, untutored fellow who arrives at his results by happy chance and good fortune. As we learn more of folk art on a worldwide basis we find more and more common characteristics that defy national boundaries. Foremost among these is training.

Like the academic artist, the folk craftsman was trained. The carvers of a fifteenth-century Gothic religious figure may be unknown, but their mastery of the medium is unquestionable. The guild system, with its rules of apprenticeship, saw to that. Nor were such regulations limited to Europe. In the Sepik River area of New Guinea, the right to carve or paint was a hereditary privilege that might be bought or sold, and apprenticeship systems existed hundreds of years ago in China and Japan.

Another important aspect of folk art is the role of the craftsman in the religious life of his community. In some primitive cultures, the painter or sculptor might actually have the status of a priest; in nearly all cases he was seen by the community as an interpreter of the will of the gods. In Polynesia, for example, it was thought that the creator of a religious carving must himself have great knowledge of the occult, for he would not otherwise be able to make figures of such power. Indians of the American West had similar beliefs about the carvers of dance masks, demonic headdresses that were believed to turn the wearer himself into a spirit. Though such beliefs were found mainly in primitive, polytheistic societies, they were not necessarily limited to them. Until fairly recently, farmers in Pennsylvania still believed in the power of the painted hex sign to protect livestock from harm, and they vied for the services of painters whose abilities to paint and to protect were felt to be particularly powerful.

Another characteristic of much folk art is that it is utilitarian. Unlike academic painting and sculpture, which exists primarily to please the eye, folk art is usually intended to do a job. A well-painted shop sign may be seen as a work of art by us, but when it was made, its purpose was simply to draw customers. A carved duck decoy may now attract collectors, but its maker sought only to attract ducks. In Polynesia, utility goes so far that painting and sculpture, far from being mere ornamentation, are thought to possess magical properties without which the decorated object, whether it be a pot or a war shield, would be useless.

Another appealing aspect of folk art is its universality. So great is man's need for self-expression that there is no culture, however poor or deprived, that cannot boast of some folk work. And as we learn more of the cross-cultural aspects of such art, it becomes evident that the concept of folk painting and sculpture as an expression of regionalism or nationalism has been somewhat exaggerated. True, there are individual art forms peculiar to certain areas, but these are subordinate to the great international stylistic movements that have periodically swept across various areas of the world.

Military conquest, of course, has had a lot to do with this. The conquering armies of Persia and Rome dragged behind them like a baggage train the folk culture and folk artists of their societies. The tastes and techniques of the victors were imposed on the vanquished, who in turn influenced their new masters. In this respect the folk-art styles of the Iberian peninsula had a profound effect on post-Columbian folk forms of South and Central America as well as on those of the southwestern United States. Likewise, the art of Japan and Korea, though it shows strong individual traits, owes much to China. Even in the scattered islands of Micronesia, in the South Pacific, one can find traces of the folk traditions carried there hundreds of years ago by canoe-borne voyagers from the coasts of southeast Asia.

Among the other factors that have influenced the development of folk art is availability of materials. In areas such as central Europe and Scandinavia, where great forests stood, wood was the material of choice. Wood could be sculpted and painted. Everything was decorated, from household furniture to religious objects, and all of it was made of wood. In areas like Iceland, where there were few trees, stone, horn, and bone were used.

In general, the more abundant the materials and the more fruitful the life of the people, the more impressive the artistic output. Not surprisingly, then, the greatest range of folk art and sculpture is found in Europe. This work is both secular and religious, with some of the most interesting work being found in the latter category.

In Italy and France one finds many votive pieces. These are paintings on wood, metal, or cloth depicting episodes in the lives of the faithful during which they felt that their lives or those of their loved ones had been spared through divine intervention. The votive pieces were given to a church as a remembrance of the occurrence. The earliest votive paintings date to the fifteenth century. They have been made in large quantities—one church, Madonna dell'Arco near Naples, has more than four thousand examples dating from the sixteenth to the twentieth centuries.

Votive pictures tend to take a standard form. At the top, a representation of the Virgin or a favored saint looks down from the clouds on the scene of the event, which may be anything from a sickbed to a train wreck. Tiny figures of the grateful suppliants raise their hands to heaven or bow in gratitude. The pieces usually also contain the date of the event, the name of the donor of the picture, and sometimes a brief description of what happened. French votive pictures, particularly those from Marseilles, are frequently quite dramatic and even gruesome in their depiction of events. The French also produced votive sculpture, including carvings of ships, planes, and automobiles, and even representations of afflicted arms or legs that had been healed through miraculous intervention. Most votive work is still in churches, but more pieces are finding their way into private collections as the sophisticated come to appreciate their strong folk quality.

Somewhat similar to these pictures are the small paintings of lost souls in torment that are found on Portuguese church collection boxes and set on poles outside country chapels. The juxtaposition of the horrors of damnation with the collection box was, no doubt, quite an effective reminder in its time!

Poland has also produced some fine religious folk painting. Until well after 1900, nearly one hundred workshops at Czestochowa were kept busy turning out oil and watercolor paintings for the many pilgrims who journeyed there to view the famous painting of the Black Virgin of Czestochowa.

Secular painting is, naturally, found in greater variety. Prior to the development of the camera, itinerant artists roamed the European countryside painting simple portraits of the local gentry. These were usually done in oil, though watercolors have been found. The most interesting of these pictures are those that can be attributed to a known artist or that incorporate period interiors and accessories. English portraits of this sort are now bringing high prices not only in the British Isles but also in America, where they may be sold as indigenous creations.

Somewhat related are the French portraits of soldiers, which were traditionally painted when the subject completed his military service. (It was considered unlucky to have the painting commissioned earlier.) These portraits usually feature the sitter in full military regalia posed against a background relating either to his branch of service or to the area in which he served. By the end of the nineteenth century these paintings had been reduced to a standard watercolor format, including a conventionalized figure on which a photograph of the soldier's head would be pasted!

Nonportrait oil paintings are of various sorts—landscapes, still lifes, or genre scenes such as depictions of local houses or farmyards. There are also, of course, animal paintings. Perhaps the best known of these are the numerous English paintings of prize cattle. During the first fifty years of the nineteenth century nearly every prosperous farmer had his ribbon-winning bull or cow painted. Most examples feature a side view of the animal, its massive outline dominating an insignificant landscape background with a low horizon line. Paintings of this sort are now extremely popular in England and Europe.

In addition to the usual canvas and board, paintings were also done on glass and other materials. Reverse-glass painting (so called because the picture is painted on the

back of a sheet of glass) was developed in Germany during the seventeenth century. Various portraits and secular or religious scenes were done in this medium. Though originally done by glaziers, these works eventually became the province of wandering peddlers. The most interesting examples come from Poland, where artists in the Carpathian Mountains added sketches of brigands and outlaws to the saints, kings, and queens found on French and German pieces. Reverse-glass painting was first brought to public attention when the Russian artist Vassily Kandinsky reproduced some examples in his *Blaue Reiter Album* of 1911.

In Scandinavia, textile and paper wall hangings were popular during the eighteenth and nineteenth centuries. Swedish artists painted them with biblical scenes or scenes of everyday life, and the subject of the painting was frequently appropriate to its owner. For example, hangings depicting the Marriage at Cana were traditionally given to newly married couples. In southern Sweden hangings were pasted to walls, but in the north the artisan would often paint them directly on the wall or even the ceiling. As is so often the case in folk pieces, most of the characters depicted, even biblical figures and others who might have lived hundreds of years earlier, were dressed in contemporary garb. The color schemes in these hangings were bold and eccentric, with blue horses, for example, being favored long before they were popularized by the modern artist Franz Marc. Nor was there any rational relationship between figures and background. In one hanging tiny figures might be lost in a forest of giant, conventionalized flowers; in another, huge subjects would tower over a diminutive landscape.

Some of the most remarkable painting has been done on wood, not only on walls and panels, but on vehicles as well. In Italy four-wheeled farm carts are ornately deco-

rated, with the composition varying from area to area. In the Emilia area of the province of Emilia-Romagna, for example, a painting of the Madonna of San Luca is traditionally found on the front board of such wagons, while St. Anthony graces the rear board. In nearby Romagna, St. Anthony gets the front board and a depiction of the Madonna of Fire is found on the rear.

While the carts on the Italian mainland are well painted, it is generally agreed that the finest work comes from Sicily. There the entire vehicle is lavishly painted and sometimes carved as well. Scenes from chivalric tales or traditional puppet plays are the most popular decorations. The Sicilian paintings seem medieval in concept, yet they could not have originated before the late eighteenth century, for before that Sicily had no roads on which the carts could travel.

Somewhat similar painted carts are found in Portugal and even in Scotland, where a "fiddle" ornament consisting of two circles or hearts and diamonds in blue and red often appears on the backboard of farm wagons from the 1850–1900 period. Of greater interest to British collectors, though, are the barge paintings of the Midlands. Until very recently, the owners of the small barges that ferried produce through the canals of central England painted their vessels inside and out. The background color was usually a strong green, with bold floral and geometric forms in red, white, scarlet, black, and yellow imposed on it. Even the boat's furnishings and water buckets were painted.

Much more delicate in nature is the fan painting of Spain and France. Skilled artists, often women, carefully embellished the paper or cloth exteriors of folding fans with complex scenes or designs in oil or watercolor. Some of the best of these have the quality of fine paintings. Most examples in this genre are from the sixteenth to nineteenth centuries.

Folk painting has even been done on canvas awnings. In France, pork butchers' shops in the 1800s and early 1900s were protected by awnings on which hunting and sporting scenes were painted. Most of this work was done in the vicinity of Lyons and Macon, and more than one example has ended up on a collector's wall.

Other painting related to commercial enterprises includes the posters put up in Italy by traveling salesmen and the sheets displayed by puppeteers and ballad singers. Puppeteers are still active in Sicily, and their vividly decorated advertisements, usually illustrating scenes from medieval romances, are fine examples of folk art. Italian merchants, like those of Germany and France, also employed catchy signs to attract customers. Among the best known are the placards used by Florentine melon vendors in the late nineteenth and early twentieth centuries.

The great importance of European folk sculpture is in large part related to the key role of woodcarving in the decoration of medieval churches. The interior of every church of any importance was ornately carved, and until well into the eighteenth century, most of the pews and other accessories were similarly decorated. Some of the finest work is among the smallest. The tiny tip-up seats that priests rested against during lengthy services were called misericordia. During the fourteenth and fifteenth centuries, the curved wooden ledges on the bottoms of these seats were carefully carved with scenes of everyday life such as sporting events and village views. Likewise, the narrow elbow rests on choir stalls were frequently carved into fanciful human and animal shapes.

Some of the men who did ecclesiastical carving, such as the great Grinling Gibbons of England (1648–1721), were honored in their time. Most, however, neither signed their work nor left any other record of creation. As a consequence, the creators of most early folk carving cannot

be identified. Ecclesiastical folk carving is widespread, however, and good examples show up in churches from Italy and Spain to Ireland and northern Scandinavia.

Most early figural sculpture, even if not made specifically for a church, was closely related to church decoration. Throughout the nineteenth century Polish craftsmen specialized in holy figures, many of which were carved from lime or oak. And even today, wood or stone figures of Christ, the Virgin, and various saints are made in the Alpine areas of Austria and Italy.

Carving was found in the home also. Fine folk carving was being done in certain areas as recently as the early twentieth century. The main gates of Rumanian houses were elaborately decorated with carved geometric devices, rosettes, and powerful linear rope patterns. In Finland, the gables of houses and the pillars supporting the ceilings were carved with motifs similar to those that once adorned Viking ships.

Some of the most interesting and collectible of all European folk carving is that relating to shop signs and symbols. In those not-so-long-ago days when most common people could not read, certain traditional symbols were associated with the various trades and crafts. Today, we think of the barber's pole and the pawnbroker's three golden balls; but two hundred years ago European streets were lined with dozens of different devices, each identifying a different shop. There were the grocer's triple sugar loaves, the hatter's top hat, the fishmonger's fish, and, for the seller of nautical instruments and sailors' gear, a jaunty midshipman in full uniform. In 1698 a French traveler named Minnon described the trade signs of London in the following terms: "They are commonly very large and jut out so far that in some narrow streets they touch one another: nay, and run across almost quite to the other side. They are generally adorned with carving and gilding

第十八拍

歸來故鄉見親族田園半蕪春草綠明燭
重然煙爐灰寒泉更洗沉泥玉載持中櫛
禮儀好一弄絲桐生死之出入闕山十二
年哀情盡在胡笳曲

and there are several which with the branches of iron that support them cost above one hundred guineas." Similar shop figures were found throughout western Europe. Some were unique to their country of origin, such as the Dutch *gapen*, the figure of a yawning man that replaced the red Indian as a sign of the tobacconist's shop in the early nineteenth century.

Inn signs, too, were quite distinctive and picturesque. In England, it was customary to use a figure related to the name of the establishment. A full-bodied, sculptured swan, for example, would mark Swan's Tavern. In Switzerland or Italy, the mountain inns had signs featuring saints, particularly those concerned with the protection of wayfarers.

As customs changed and literacy increased, many of these signs were discarded. Sometimes their removal was dictated by law, as in England, where local officials were instructed to remove them in 1762. The signs had simply become too numerous. Most that were taken down were destroyed, but a surprising number have made their way into private collections. The major problem faced by today's collector is avoiding the all too numerous fake and reproduced signs that have appeared as demand has increased.

Other examples of eagerly sought folk carving include ships' figureheads and various circus or fair figures. Figureheads were a "must" as adornments for the prows of sailing vessels, but with the advent of the steel-hulled ship in the late nineteenth century they went the way of the dodo. Some have been preserved, but because of their great size (as much as 15 feet [4.6 m] in length) and the difficulty of removing them from the ships' hulls, most of them were destroyed. Today, unfortunately, they are rather rare. Circus figures are easier to come by. The human and animal figures associated with carousels and

those carved to decorate circus wagons and tents have, within the past decade, become valuable collectors' items, though most are not very old. Workshops in the vicinity of Angers in France were making such objects in quantity as late as 1895, and in some out-of-the-way parts of Europe circus figures continued to be carved by hand until the Second World War.

Many smaller secular carvings may also be found. The Oberammergau and Berchtesgaden areas of Germany are famous for their nineteenth-century woodcarvings. These include Christmas pyramids (the forerunner of the Christmas tree) decorated with biblical characters and miners, as well as wooden models of ships and mining scenes constructed inside glass bottles.

Though thought of as being more appropriate to primitive societies, the carving of ritual masks is still practiced in remote areas of Europe. In the Appenzell and Sargans regions of Switzerland an ancient play is performed at dusk on January 13th, the eve of the Feast of Sylvesterkläuse (New Year's Day in the Old Style calendar). The actors, who represent the forces of good and evil, wear grotesque carved masks and clash in battle, shrieking and ringing cowbells. The evil forces are always vanquished, and the victory heralds a prosperous new year. Masks are also carved, painted, and worn in Sicily and in the mountainous regions of Italy and Yugoslavia during the pre-Lenten carnival. These masks are typically demonic or bestial in aspect.

One other type of folk carving should be mentioned—the gravestone. In many areas of Europe great respect was paid to the deceased by crowning his or her grave with an elaborate headstone. Irish stones of the eighteenth and nineteenth centuries have a central carving depicting the Crucifixion, with the symbols of the Passion—ladder, spear, pincers, and hammer—ranged symmetrically about

明太祖真像

帝名元璋朱姓江南句容人在位三十一年號洪武

it. In Yugoslavia, more attention is focused on the individual: his portrait and various pious sayings alluding to his life and works are carved into the headstone. Obtaining rubbings or impressions in ink of old gravestones has become a popular hobby.

Folk art in the New World has tended to follow the forms and techniques of the colonizing countries, but with certain differences. Folk painting, for example, is far more important in the United States than in England. In the United States, a dearth of academic painters, combined with a nationalistic pride (particularly in New England) in doing things oneself, led to a proliferation of folk painters. American collectors were attracted to folk art earlier than most Europeans, and they have discovered the works of hundreds of indigenous painters. Most of these were portrait painters who traveled through the Northeast and Midwest, setting up studios for brief periods in small towns or in farmhouses. There they would paint portraits quickly and inexpensively.

The work of some of these men has attracted attention in Europe as well as in the United States. Such painters as Rufus Porter and Joseph Whitney Stock are almost as well known In London as they are in New York. Porter (1792–1884) is almost a prototype of the American folk painter. His long life spanned the most productive period in folk art, and his career was typical. Born in Boxford, Massachusetts, Porter followed successively the careers of shoemaker, fife and violin player, schoolteacher, inventor, house and sign painter, and, finally, portrait and landscape painter. He worked and he traveled, and he never made much money. One of his paintings will sell today for more than he made in his entire lifetime.

Some of the most interesting American folk artists were not portrait painters, however. As the country expanded, the need for documenting that growth offered many op-portunities for other kinds of artists. While they occasionally painted purely decorative landscapes, more often regional artists were called on to depict specific scenes. Folk artists recorded the building of the mills of New England, the opening of the western lands, and the growth of the railroads that bound the sprawling country together.

The perfection of the camera gradually put an end to most folk painters, but in one area, at least, the artist held his place into the twentieth century. That was ship painting. As American fleets swarmed across the seas in the early 1800s, sea captains and ship owners grew rich—and they all wanted paintings of their vessels. Literally thousands of American seascapes and ship paintings are known, many of them by identifiable artists. Among the better known of these are the Bard brothers of New York State's Hudson Valley and Antonio Jacobson of New York City. Jacobson (1850–1921) was extremely prolific. His journals record the painting of some two thousand works, and it is generally agreed that he probably executed twice that number. It is said that when he had to, he could paint a piece in a single day. Jacobson seems to have done a painting of every U.S. vessel of the 1870–1910 period, as well as many foreign-flag vessels.

Oil and watercolor paintings of trains, early automobiles, balloons, and the like are less common. The great documenters in these areas were the lithographers. The best-known American lithographers are Nathaniel Currier and James. M. Ives. Active throughout the second half of the nineteenth century, Currier and Ives recorded nearly every facet of American life of their day, from bucolic country scenes to Civil War battles. Though they have been widely reproduced, original Currier and Ives lithographs are in great demand and command very substantial prices—in most cases, well in excess of what one would pay for an original academic painting of the period.

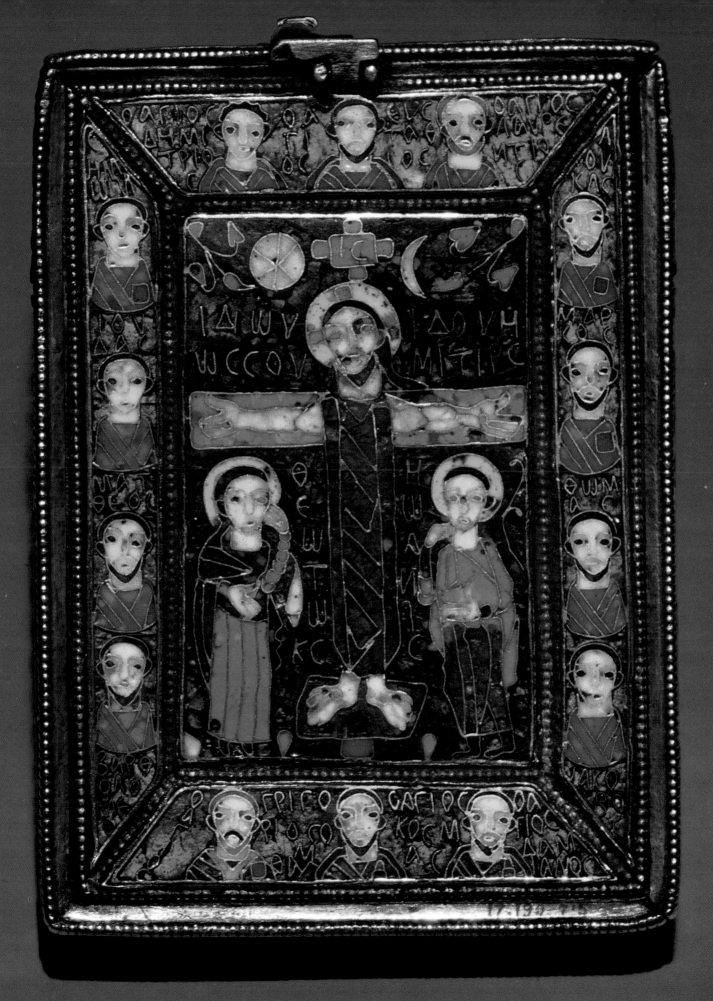

Since the United States was the most rapidly industrialized of all nations, one would imagine that folk painting would have vanished first here. Quite the contrary. Even in this century folk artists flourish, and collectors eagerly seek out their work. Such painters as the celebrated Grandma Moses have, even in their own lifetimes, seen their work exceed in value that of many contemporary academic painters. Folk painting remains very much alive and well in twentieth-century America.

The folk sculpture of the United States is less varied than that of Europe. Good, authentic inn signs and carved storekeepers' figures, in great demand among collectors, are increasingly hard to come by. Without a doubt, the American favorite is the cigar-store Indian. Though carvers like Samuel Robb of New York City were turning out hundreds of these in the late nineteenth century, most are now gone. No more than three thousand authentic American shop figures are believed to exist. Unfortunately, the fakes and copies well exceed this number.

Other folk figures made in the United States include ships' figureheads, carousel figures, and individual sculptures of everything from Indians to Abraham Lincoln. These latter were in some cases carved to decorate public buildings, in others as diversion for their creators.

Unlike Europe, the United States has produced relatively little folk sculpture and painting of a religious nature, and the few examples that exist are not of much interest to collectors. The *santos*, or saints' figures, of the Southwest are the most important religious sculpture, and these are strongly Spanish in influence. Religious paintings, where found, are generally disregarded, and even the few religious prints done by Currier and Ives are practically unsalable.

Some of the very finest folk painting and sculpture comes from Africa and Polynesia. These tropical areas

with a pastoral, technologically primitive population have produced a plethora of extraordinary art. As previously mentioned, much of this art had a religious purpose.

In Africa the secret societies—men's organizations that dominated nearly every facet of tribal life, from government to family planning—staged elaborate ritual dances and meetings. They required large numbers of masks for such rites, and a major function of tribal carvers was to provide these masks. In the Belgian Congo (now Zaire) the Bwame society in the Leopoldville (now Kinshasa) area employed extraordinarily sophisticated carved ivory masks. Bone, leather, and other materials were also used in maskmaking, but for the most part, the preferred material was wood. The African carver worked slowly but carefully and with precision, often taking several months to complete a single mask. Most were carved in the round, and many were painted. The form was basically abstract, for the artist sought to capture the essence or "spirit" of the object portrayed rather than its actual appearance. And, of course, many of the masks were intended to represent deities, making it even less likely that they would take a realistic form.

African masks did not come to the attention of the western world until well after 1850, and most major collections have been gathered since that time. Craftsmen in this vast area have continued to work, both for their own use and to provide for a growing collector trade. As a consequence, African masks and sculpture (for the artisans also carve many full figures) are still readily available in Europe and North America. Since these are made in Africa, even if they are contemporary or only a few years old, they cannot be called fakes or even reproductions. However, it does appear that there has been a steady decline in quality over the past few decades. Too many artists today are working only for sale, and the religious and cultural factors that once motivated them are now largely dissipated.

Much the same phenomenon occurred at an earlier date in the Pacific islands. The vast area known as Polynesia has a strong artistic tradition. Since wood was the most available material, most Polynesian artists were wood-carvers, though they also turned out some remarkable paintings on wood and fiber. If anything, Polynesian art was even more abstract than that of Africa. In an area beset by natural calamities ranging from typhoons to volcanic eruptions, a strong need for divine assistance was felt, and almost all Polynesian art was created as an appeal to the gods. Strong, geometric forms with intricate carving and bold decoration in flat planes of color predominate. Masks for ritual dances and statues of local gods are common, but equally important are the carvings that cover weapons, house posts and gables, and canoe prows. All of these are intended to make magic—to enable the owner of the weapon to strike surely, to assure the swift and safe return of the canoe.

The introduction of Christianity and western customs had a devastating effect on Polynesian folk art. With a much smaller area and population, the islands lacked the cultural resilience of Africa and (with the exception of certain areas such as New Guinea) were quickly converted to western ways. There has been little Polynesian folk art of any consequence since before the First World War.

China and Japan have had such sophisticated societies for so long that it is almost arbitrary to define anything made there as folk art. Nevertheless, certain types of art are thought of as being of the people. In Japan, this would certainly include the woodblock print. From the early eighteenth century on, Japanese artists have carved remarkable blocks from which multiple copies can be made. These prints, usually done on rice paper, are of familiar scenes: teahouses, actors and musicians at work, famous natural sites such as Mt. Fuji, and so on. Many artists have made woodblock prints, but certain names stand out. Ando Hiroshige (1797–1858) and Katsushika Hokusai (1760–1849) are generally regarded as the greatest workers in the genre. Hokusai's *Thirty-seven Views of Fuji* is regarded as a masterpiece, and original or early prints are eagerly sought by collectors. Hiroshige is best known for his lovely landscape views of *The Fifty-three Stations of the Tokaido.*

Japanese folk sculpture is primarily of a religious nature. Priests were practically required to be sculptors themselves. The combination of a damp climate and various natural disasters resulted in constant damage to temple figures, and most temple sculpture has been made over in whole or in part many times during the past centuries. As temples closed, many smaller figures were dispersed, and it is not difficult to obtain these carvings.

In both China and India there were schools of folk painting. Though the woodblock print was employed, Chinese and Indian artists worked primarily in watercolors. Chinese watercolors were often topical, dealing with historical events and tales of the nobility; Indian genre painting tended to focus more on religious themes. The Indian miniature paintings of the seventeenth and eighteenth centuries are particularly prized by western collectors. The bright colors and gilding of these works, as well as the fanciful themes—heroes and mythical monsters—are extremely appealing.

The nature of folk art is so inclusive and its themes are so pervasive in every culture that the serious collector can find examples virtually everywhere. One need only look. It is, therefore, hardly surprising that folk-art collecting is one of the fastest-growing fields in the world of antiques.

2
Furniture

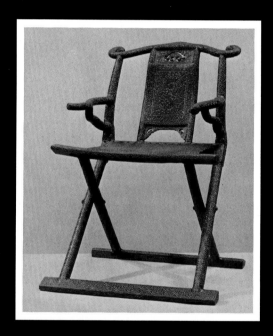

Preceding pp.: American Victorian
sitting room, 1870s. The furnishings, though of
high quality, are primarily factory made.
Above: Japanese lacquered wood folding chair, 16th
century. The "X" or scissors chair,
adapted from Chinese models, is one of the few
chair forms indigenous to Japan.

By far the greatest variety and quantity of antique furnishings are found in western Europe and those areas of the Americas where European colonies were established. England, France, Germany, Holland, Italy, Spain, and Portugal have long been great furnituremaking centers; but as one travels north, east, or south, the volume of available material drops sharply.

Collectors of European and North American furniture, faced as they are with an overwhelming breadth of choice, often do not realize that in many other areas of the world very little old furniture is available. In some cases, as with China, this lack of examples reflects the destruction resulting from war and natural calamities, but in far more instances it is a manifestation of choice. People simply did not use much furniture prior to the modern era.

The type and amount of household furnishings used in a given society are based on many things: the climate, the type of home occupied, the available raw materials, the life style of the people. Life style can be particularly important. Wanderers, for example, do not own wardrobes. The nomadic tribes of northern Africa and the Near East have always lived on the move, traveling from one oasis or grazing area to another. Large pieces of furniture do not fit well on a camel or a donkey cart. In such areas small chests, often elaborately decorated, and low stools are almost the only furniture found; carpets and rugs are regarded as of much greater importance.

The earliest western furniture we know of is that used in ancient Greece, Rome, and Egypt. From the few remaining pieces, most of which were found in tombs or in houses buried by volcanic eruptions, it is evident that the craftsmen of these societies were familiar with sophisticated cabinetmaking techniques. Many of the skills used in creating such pieces were lost during the Dark Ages following the collapse of the Roman Empire. Isolated from Egypt and Byzantium, where skilled cabinetmaking still flourished, the craftsmen of western Europe almost had to relearn their craft.

The style created during this period of relearning (500–1100 A.D.) is known as the Romanesque. Following the collapse of the western Roman Empire in the fifth century, cabinetmakers in Europe employed a style based on remembered forms of Roman decoration, relying primarily on crudely carved plant and animal motifs. Chaotic living conditions during the Romanesque period did not encourage furnituremaking, and the little we know of this period has been gleaned from surviving writings, paintings, and sculpture. It appears that chests, chairs, and some beds were made, but all are now gone.

By the thirteenth century, however, conditions in western Europe had stabilized somewhat. Nation-states were developing, and with them a class of nobles with the prerogatives of nobility, including luxurious furnishings. But the dominant cultural force was the church, and the chief artistic expression of the new age (known to us as the Gothic) was ecclesiastical. The cathedral was the triumph of Gothic art, and the stonemason was its artist. Furnituremaking during this period (1200–1400), though much advanced over the previous era, trailed behind and copied architecture.

This was due in part to the fact that architectural techniques were more advanced at the time, in part to the nature of the people and the character of their homes. The rich and high-born, the only ones who could afford much furniture in the Gothic era, were peripatetic in the extreme. In the Middle Ages it was customary for the nobility, rather than occupying a single dwelling, to travel from house to house within their holdings. Such a life, like that of the distant Bedouins, discouraged the use of bulky furnishings. The chief furnishings to come down to

Below: Italian *cassone*, or chest,
16th century. The *cassone* was the most important
piece of Renaissance furniture, and
famous artists of the period often painted or
carved it. This northern Italian
example is decorated with carved allegorical
figures. Opposite: French cupboard
in the Baroque style, 16th century. The lush
carving and ball feet on this piece
are typical of French Baroque furniture. The
style was so popular that it
lingered for 200 years in provincial areas.

us from the thirteenth and fourteenth centuries are chests of various sizes. They were portable and useful for anything from storage to sitting. A few chairs may also be found, but they are rare and primarily of the folding sort that were used centuries before by Roman generals on campaigns.

Another factor militating against much furniture was the way in which medieval living space was used. The traditional center of activity in the great houses of the rich and powerful was the hall, a large open space constantly in use for everything from state banquets to routine domestic activities. Meals were served here, counsel taken, and punishments meted out. When the day's activities were over, the participants, like as not, curled up on the floor for a night's rest. Since so many people gathered there, the central floor of the hall had to be kept clear. Consequently, there was little furniture. Large storage chests might be ranged along the walls, and these frequently served as chairs, tables, and even beds. Cupboards and true beds, where they existed, were built into the walls; tables were made of boards mounted on trestles so that they could be taken apart when not in use.

Construction and decoration of Gothic furniture became more sophisticated as the period progressed. The earliest Gothic chests were constructed just as they had been in the Romanesque period. Wooden planks were chopped out with an axe and nailed together with hand-made nails or bound with wrought-iron straps. As cathe-

dral-building developed, however, cabinetmakers adopted the architectural device of the skeleton framework and applied it to the construction of chests and cupboards. First a sturdy rectangular framework was built, then thin wooden panels were fitted into slots in this framework. The resultant furnishings were not only lighter but also stronger.

Gothic furniture was invariably made of oak. Sometimes it was simply polished; more often, it was carved as well. The inspiration for carved decoration came primarily from church architecture. The pointed arches, pillars, and buttresses of the great churches were reduced in scale and faithfully copied in wood. Floral forms such as vines and leaves were popular, as were grotesque animal and human forms mimicking the gargoyles that adorned the eaves of the great houses of worship.

Because it is a very hard wood that splinters easily, oak allows for only large-scale and relatively simple carving. Toward the end of the Gothic period, artisans seeking more elaborate forms of decoration turned to painting and gilding. Again they looked to the church for inspiration—the decorative motifs used on much late Gothic painted furniture bear a distinct resemblance to those found in illuminated manuscripts of the period.

Romanesque and to a greater extent Gothic furniture was produced in greatest quantity in northern Europe. Many basic forms, of course, were corrupt versions of classic Roman furnishings adapted to local conditions by the Germanic conquerors of the Empire, but the northern tribes did more than copy. They transformed the classic lines and motifs of Greco-Roman architecture and furniture into an angular and geometric art distinctly their own.

Italians did not greet this new style with enthusiasm, and the Gothic mode made little headway in southern Europe. What passes for Italian Gothic is little more than the imposition of a few northern motifs on a taste that remained basically classic. As the seafaring city-states of Italy grew rich on trade and increased their contact with the nations bordering the eastern Mediterranean, they began to evolve a new style based in part on their Greco-Roman heritage (what we term the classic) and in part on Moorish forms that reached them through Constantinople, which until the middle of the fifteenth century was the capital of the eastern Roman Empire.

The newly popular fashion was known as the Renaissance, and its tremendous impact on European arts and crafts occurred during the period between 1400 and 1550. The Renaissance, or "rebirth," was viewed at the time as a harkening back to the lost glories of ancient Greece and Rome. In actuality, it was a period of momentous advances in all areas of human activity, from science to politics to the arts.

Design and decoration are the hallmarks of Renaissance furniture and the key to its importance in European social development. The Italian designers and their followers turned the world around. Whereas Romanesque and Gothic cabinetmakers had worked almost exclusively in oak, a strong wood but difficult to carve and totally unsuited to inlay or veneering, Renaissance artisans turned to walnut, ebony, and other woods. Whereas prior styles had been limited either by construction methods or by lack of creative imagination, the new wave excelled in both. Cabinetmakers universally adopted framing as the construction method of choice, and on the stronger and lighter base framing provided they lavished a variety of decoration unknown in prior eras. With the development of water-powered sawmills they were able to turn structural elements on a lathe and thereby produce rounded legs and arms instead of the previously hand-carved pieces.

Decoration became varied and complex. Through their contacts with Islamic states, both Italy and Spain discovered Moorish techniques such as intarsia, the inlay in wood of substances such as bone and metal. From the Near East also came design motifs such as the star, the crescent, and the intertwining scrollwork known as the arabesque. Forbidden by their religion to use the human form as a decorative device, the Moors had developed naturalistic and geometric forms to a high state, and Renaissance craftsmen eagerly adapted these for their own use.

The Renaissance was also a period of great artistic advances, and both painters and sculptors of the day worked on furniture. Piero di Cosimo and other well-known artists of the time painted chests or carved the backs for couches. In fact, by the end of the Renaissance many cabinetmakers had themselves attained the status of artists, and their creations, no longer merely utilitarian, were now seen as works of art.

To a great extent, the new forms and styles of furniture developed during the Renaissance reflected changes in people's life styles. By the beginning of the fifteenth century, the nobility had stopped going on the Grand Tour each year and settled into permanent dwellings, the nature of which also underwent modification. The central hall was replaced by various living spaces, including bedrooms, and furniture was designed to suit these. The chest was given legs to raise it above the damp stone floors, and drawers to make it more accessible. Other furnishings were also developed to meet the needs of a society that was both more sedentary and more prosperous.

Since the Renaissance originated in Italy it is not surprising that many of the new furniture forms developed there. From the Gothic chest, Italian artisans developed the *cassone*, a very large, elaborate storage container. Some *cassoni* were as much as 8 feet (2.4 m) long and all were lavishly decorated. Since people had been sitting and sleeping on chests for years, it was also quite logical for the craftsmen of Florence and Naples to add a back and arms to it, transforming it into the *cassapanca*, a forerunner of today's sofa. Though it could have been an entirely independent creation, the *cassapanca* closely resembled the *kang*, a much earlier Chinese bedlike couch; it is not unlikely that examples or descriptions of the *kang* reached Italy through Near Eastern sources.

New chairs and tables were also designed. Venetian cabinetmakers developed the *sgabello*, a portable chair that was little more than a stool with a back. Since it was easily movable, the *sgabello* was well suited to the Renaissance house, which had many rooms. The Italians also modified the ancient "X" or scissors chair. For centuries it had been collapsible so that it might be used by people traveling about the country. Since life was now more stable, it became a piece of rigid furniture covered with leather and rich brocades.

New furnishings were also developed in other countries to suit the needs and tastes of the people. In Spain, where the Renaissance style was referred to as the Plateresque, the chest acquired a slanted drop front and became a desk, the *vargueño*. The Renaissance came early to Spain, for it was both politically and religiously close to Italy. However, furniture of the Spanish Renaissance was quite different from that of Italy. As in other places, tables were no longer made to be taken apart after each meal, but Spanish tables were more massive and were bound together by beautiful wrought-iron stretchers. In fact, the use of iron, from decorative nailheads to bedposts, was characteristic of Spanish furniture of this period.

The Renaissance mode dominated France during the reign of François I (1515–1547), rapidly replacing Gothic architecture and furniture, which had reached a high state of development. A variety of tables appeared, all with bases richly carved in the Italian manner. Chairs became more comfortable and began to replace stools and benches. Cushions were used over the bare wood, and rush-bottomed chairs arrived on the scene in the late sixteenth century. People no longer wanted to fold clothing and pack it in horizontal chests, so the standing clothes cupboard, or "press," was developed. Many of these richly carved pieces were very large, and they dominated any room in which they were placed.

Renaissance influences spread slowly into northern Europe, where they were integrated with decorative and structural techniques retained from the Gothic period. In Germany and Holland, Renaissance-style carving was more exuberant and lavish than in the South, particularly in the massive cupboards and elaborately decorated four-poster beds produced in these areas. In England, King Henry VIII employed Italian architects and designers who introduced Renaissance decorative motifs, but for the most part English cabinetmakers kept on making the same type of furniture they had made during the Gothic era. It was just decorated differently now.

By the middle of the sixteenth century, the Renaissance spirit, though still finding converts in the more isolated areas of Europe, was largely spent in Italy. The balance and basic simplicity of what was essentially a classic mode was not elaborate enough for many, and a new style gradually emerged. This was the Baroque (1550–1700). Baroque furniture reflected a great emphasis on decoration and less concern with form. Though initially Italian in inspiration, the style was most fully developed by the French, and this fact heralded the replacement of Italy by France as the center of European furniture design.

Baroque furniture was characterized by exaggerated size, scale, and proportion. Lavish carving was typical, as

(1) French Louis XV lady's dressing table, 18th century. This view from above shows the remarkable marquetry work on the top of this piece. (2) French Louis XV sofa, *c.* 1770. This piece is well carved and typical of fine French overstuffed furniture. (3) French *secrétaire*, or drop-front desk, designed by J. H. Riesener, 18th century. This desk is decorated with marquetry and ormolu mounts. (4) French Louis XV lady's writing desk, 18th century. The veneered surfaces and cabriole legs of this piece are quite appealing.

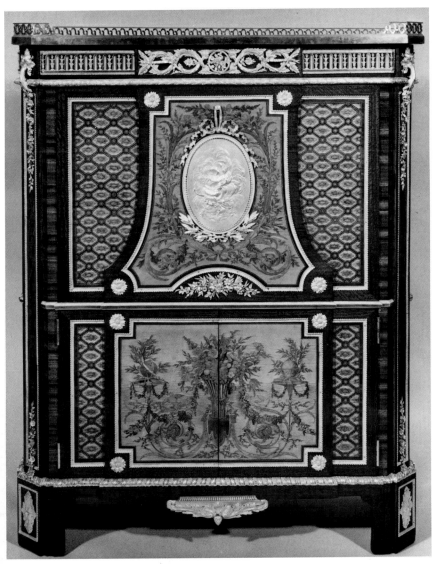

4

was unorthodox treatment of accepted Renaissance features. Pediments became tremendous in relation to the pieces they crowned, scrollwork became large and twisted, and moldings deepened to achieve spectacular effects of light and shade. Inlays of brilliant materials such as gilt, marble, and bronze contributed to a rich effect beneath which the original form of the piece vanished.

New forms of furniture were developed. The *cassone* was superseded by console tables and wall seats. Cabinets became even larger, with sculptured bases and elaborate carvings of eagles, lions, and blackamoors. Veneering—the application of thin sheets of attractively grained wood over plain wood—became popular, as did the use of marble and other stone for tabletops. Chairs had flowing outlines and were covered with stamped leather and decorated with nailheads, in the Spanish manner.

In France, Louis XIV tired of importing Italian cabinetwork and set out to create the first government-controlled and -directed style. He transformed the old Gobelin tapestry factory into a royal furniture manufactory and brought both patronage and control to the cabinetmakers. The French accepted the Baroque wholeheartedly and embellished it with their own creations. New forms were developed. The commode, a two-drawer chest on legs, became an important decorative storage piece. French designers also developed the sofa, an upholstered piece suitable to the luxurious tastes of the period.

Cabinetmakers from all over Europe hastened to Paris, and the new style enveloped Europe. In Holland the new mode manifested itself in sumptuous carving. High-backed caned chairs of almost thronelike quality appeared, as did the *kas*, an enormous clothes press with massive moldings and painted decoration.

Similar cabinets were made in the Germanic states, but there the decoration was much more French in feeling.

2

1

3

The cabinetmakers of Hamburg and Frankfurt built monumental cupboards with large, ball-like feet and lushly carved decorative patterns featuring leaf, flower, and fruit ornaments. Their chairs and tables had turned spiral legs; and tables and cabinet pieces were frequently inlaid with wood or metal. In fact, marquetry, the inlay of wood in contrasting light and dark shades, reached its greatest sophistication in Germany at this time.

The Baroque did not reach England until Charles II returned from exile in Flanders in 1660. He brought with him workmen from the court of Louis XIV, and they introduced the lush movement of the Baroque to England. This period (1660–1688), called the Restoration in England, saw the development of many forms new to the British Isles. Daybeds, desks, sofas, and wing chairs appeared here for the first time.

English Baroque decoration followed that of France with deep-cut, flowing carving, marquetry, and the use of caning, upholstering, rich hangings, and stamped leather. Veneering was popular, and the English invented oystering, the use of cross sections of small branches as veneer.

Trade with the Far East had increased greatly by this time, and as a major seafaring power, England enjoyed the riches of the East. Chinese and Japanese lacquerware, made by the tedious application and polishing of countless layers of shellac, was all the rage, and lacquered furniture appeared both here and in Holland. Oriental themes were also employed in the painting and gilding of furniture.

Despite its elaborate decoration, the Baroque never lost its link to the classicism of the Renaissance. Compositions, though confused, at least remained symmetrical. Such was not the case in the following period. The Rococo (1700–1770), named for the rocks (*rocailles*) that were used to decorate the gardens of Versailles, was based on a light and extravagantly free-flowing naturalism that

4

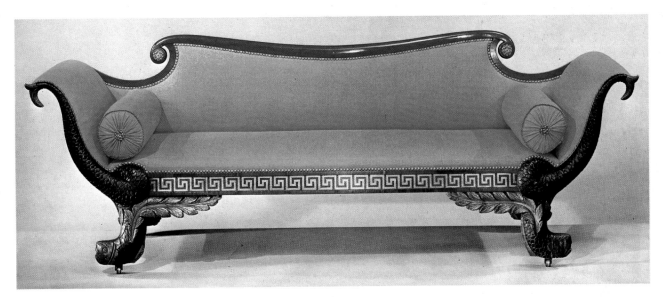

emphasized curved, irregular forms. Rococo pieces are typically asymmetrical and lushly decorated with flora and fauna motifs. Surface decoration, including gilding, painting, carving, and application of gilt-bronze (ormolu) ornaments almost totally obscures the outlines of individual pieces of furniture.

French dominance in design continued unabated during the Rococo. Many authorities feel that the decorative furniture of the Louis XV period is the finest ever made, and without doubt it is extraordinary. Only flowing lines were used, and everything was rounded so that the eye could follow any line without ever perceiving a junction of planes. Decoration, whether paint, marquetry, or metal, was applied with the eye of an artist, for, indeed, the French craftsmen had become artists.

In keeping with the curvilinear style of the times, table and chair legs acquired a new shape, an "S" curve known as the cabriole and fashioned to resemble the form of an animal's leg. In keeping with social habits and costumes, seats were built low, with low backs. In an age when the upper classes were enjoying great luxury and much leisure time, tables appropriate for various card and dice games appeared, as did many different types of dressing tables and a slant-front desk adapted from the commode.

The Rococo had its greatest effect on Germany during the period from 1730 to 1790. French furniture and French artisans were imported, and carving, gilding, and painting in the French manner were extremely popular. Germanic artisans went further than their masters in some respects. Their furniture shows more unrestrained fantasy, with the employment of bright, almost garish paint, an exaggerated cabriole leg, and swelling bombé fronts for secretaries, cupboards, and chests of drawers.

The Dutch also accepted the Rococo, though with less

enthusiasm, and by the time the style reached England, its contributions were limited to the cabriole leg and the embellishment of gilt mirrors. For the English had now developed their own modes and never again followed closely those of the Continent.

The cabriole leg, accepted during the reign of Queen Anne (1702–1714), was applied with great taste to sleek, splat-back chairs and tall chests on stands known as highboys. Ornamentation was subordinated in favor of fine woods such as walnut and the rich mahogany becoming available from the West Indies. Considering the lavish gilding and painting of France, English decoration of the period seems modest in the extreme.

In the course of the following Georgian period (1714–1795) more elaborate decoration appeared. Carving reasserted itself, and the cabriole leg now ended not in a simple pad but in a hoof shape or a ball-and-claw form derived from the Oriental motif of the guardian dragon clutching the Jewel of Buddha. There was greater emphasis on detail, spurred largely by the publication in 1754 of *The Gentleman and Cabinet-Maker's Director* by Thomas Chippendale. Chippendale, a furnituremaker and designer, created a book of patterns based on a mixture of late Baroque and Rococo types mingled with Gothic and Chinese details. Chippendale's version of the Rococo differed sharply from that of the Continent, for even where *rocaille* work or fretwork in the Chinese manner appeared, it was always subordinated to a strong outline. Form was never lost.

Nor could form remain forever lost in Europe. By the middle of the eighteenth century both consumers and designers were yearning for a return to straight lines and simple forms. Excavations at the ancient, long-buried cities of Herculaneum and Pompeii had revealed the classic forms and decorative styles prevalent in the last great period of the Roman Empire. After the excesses of the Rococo, these mathematically symmetrical forms appeared to be the essence of purity.

The earliest prominent exponents of the new mode, which came to be termed the Classic Revival (1770–1810), were Robert and James Adam, a pair of Scottish architects. Robert visited the rediscovered city of Herculaneum in the 1750s, and when he returned to England he immediately set about re-creating in architecture, furniture, and the decorative arts the glory that was Rome. The Adam brothers sought to create complete interiors, all in the same classic manner, so they employed all sorts of craftsmen—cabinetmakers, smiths, weavers, and so on.

Among those associated with the Adam group were two renowned English cabinetmakers, George Hepplewhite and Thomas Sheraton, each of whom gave his name to a type of furniture. Both stressed strong vertical and horizontal lines combined with delicate construction and flat panels that could be decorated with veneer or paint. Hepplewhite preferred tapered legs ending in square blocks and chairs with round or shield-shaped backs; Sheraton is known for round, reeded legs and rectangular backs.

The Classic Revival came later to France, in part because Louis XV preferred the Rococo. With Louis XVI's ascension to the throne in 1774, however, French architects and cabinetmakers were allowed to give full reign to their new ideas. The asymmetrical and foliate decoration of the prior period quickly vanished, to be replaced by form and decoration based on ancient architectural remains. Fluting and grooving emphasized verticals; moldings and feet were modeled after the capitals and bases of Roman columns. The heavy carving and raised decoration of the Rococo were superseded by flat panels and narrow moldings. Classical ornamental devices such as oak leaves and Greek palms and urns appeared, while brass and gilt, if used at all, were used on a delicate, small scale.

German classicism was greatly influenced by English
and French prototypes. The straight lines were adopted,
but ornamentation was more florid, a characteristic of previous periods as well. A variety of interesting pieces
including desks, commodes, and writing tables were designed by David Roentgen, the leading German designer
of the period and one of the best in all Europe.

Italy, ironically, almost missed the Classic Revival. It
was not until the end of the eighteenth century that Italian artisans began to copy Adam, Sheraton, and Louis XVI
designs. The furniture they produced differed from that of
northern Europe in that it was less formal and more richly
decorated, primarily with gilding, paint, marquetry, and
marble. Perhaps the best-known examples of the era are
the Milanese commodes that are inlaid with various light-
colored woods.

When Napoleon Bonaparte took power in France in
1804 he helped promote a continuation of the Classic Revival that became known as Empire. The new mode differed from that realized under Louis XVI in that its
proponents absorbed classic forms whole rather than using their elements to create something new. In this sense
the style was a definite step backward. The Napoleonic
designers took the few available examples of Greco-Roman furniture and copied them exactly; then, finding that
there were no ancient equivalents for most furnishings in
use in the early nineteenth century, they simply made up
what seemed appropriate and applied existent archaic
forms and decorations.

Absolute symmetry, heavy, solid proportions, and large,
flat surfaces free of molding or decoration characterize
this furniture. Ornamentation, where it exists, consists
almost exclusively of applied fixtures in gilt or bronze.
Other than on the arms of chairs and legs of tables, carving
disappeared.

American rosewood bed by John Belter, New York City, *c.* 1860. This bed, in the Empire style, is made of laminated wood in a technique largely developed by Belter, one of the earliest and most successful exponents of industrialized furnituremaking. Through the use of lamination he was able to produce stronger and more decorative furniture at considerably less expense. His pieces are in great demand today among American collectors.

Most Empire furniture is massive and rather uncomfortable. Chairs and sofas, even when upholstered, managed to make the sitter squirm; but beds, particularly the boat-shaped sleigh bed with upswept head- and footboards, were interesting.

The Empire style was imposed on Italy and Germany by Napoleon's conquering armies. Italian manifestations of the style exhibited little national character and were practically interchangeable with French examples. The mode had staying power, though, and it remained the basic Italian style throughout most of the nineteenth century, for Victorian fashions had little impact here.

In Germany matters took a different course. Even at its worst, German Empire was lighter, with smooth veneered surfaces and a livable quality. Around 1830 it evolved into the Biedermeier style, which featured furniture of a distinctly classical turn but light in weight and color—a definite contrast to the brooding Empire. Instead of the usual walnut, light-colored native woods such as birch, apple, and cherry were used, and decoration, based on floral and animal motifs, was graceful and delicate. Chairs and sofas were more curvilinear than most Empire furniture, and much easier to live with.

The manifestation of Empire in England was known as Regency (1800–1837), a term relating to the period when George, Prince of Wales, served as Regent. Though they did not copy Continental pieces, English Regency furnituremakers did share the intense desire to re-create archeologically exact copies of Greco-Roman artifacts. Furnishings were made of walnut or mahogany with broad, undecorated surfaces enlivened by brass or gilt fittings carefully copied from locks, handles, and the like found on pieces in the Italian excavations.

With the exception of pieces by well-known designers, European Empire furniture remains virtually undiscovered by collectors and substantially underpriced. Good examples, particularly in the German Biedermeier style, will prove valuable acquisitions.

At the end of the 1830s cabinetmakers abandoned the Empire-Regency style for an eclectic approach involving the use of design elements from prior periods. These elements were combined in furniture as the craftsmen saw fit, with the only common element a great emphasis on elaborate decoration. Since this period largely coincided with the reign of England's Queen Victoria, it was known as the Victorian era (1840–1910).

Early Victorian was based on the late Empire, with some elements of Sheraton and a lot of Gothic derivative detail added. The woods used were primarily mahogany and walnut. In the middle period French furnishings of the Rococo-Louis XV era were revived, though scale and curvature were exaggerated. At this time cabinetmaking began to feel the full effects of industrialization. Machine-cut parts, steam-pressed design, and elaborately turned structural members began to replace handwork. Furniture was now manufactured in shops, with each man generally working on a small part of a piece of furniture. Most of these workers had little understanding of the overall design of the furniture they were creating. As a result, design coherency began to break down.

In the late Victorian period (after 1870) Renaissance details and rectilinear shapes appeared, often in combination with Gothic details. At this point oak replaced walnut as the favored wood, and design became a factory product, with individual designers retiring from the scene. Efficiency became the keynote in furniture design, and factories produced a plethora of combination pieces: bed-wardrobes, table-chests, desk-bookcases, and the like.

Toward the end of the Victorian era, William Morris, an English artist, poet, and architect, led a movement in

reaction to machine manufacture. The Arts and Crafts movement, as it came to be known, extended to all areas of the decorative and utilitarian arts—metalware, glass, textiles, as well as furniture—and represented a desire to return to the careful craftsmanship of the Middle Ages. The furniture built in Morris's workshops was functional, made of plain oak, and vaguely Gothic in style. Not only was it relatively undecorated, but it was almost entirely handmade, which was really a swim against the tide at that time. The Arts and Crafts movement attracted little attention outside England and the United States, but it laid the groundwork for much subsequent European and American design theory.

Victorian eclecticism did not affect Europe with the same intensity evident in England and the United States. In Italy it barely existed, in Germany it was confined to a revival of Renaissance and Empire motifs oddly mixed with additions from Turkey and the Near East. France survived a brief revival of the Gothic before plunging into another Renaissance revival (the Second Empire, 1852–1870), which was followed at the end of the century by the Art Nouveau style, based on an elaboration of the Rococo in a mode emphasizing organic forms. The first great French stylist of the period was Emile Gallé (1846–1904). In a 1900 article for a French review, he clearly stated the difference between traditional Victorian furniture and Art Nouveau when he declared that "as for the shape of limbs, one can either adopt traditional shapes, which leaves little scope for fantasy, or draw one's inspiration from the shape of plants."

Much Art Nouveau furniture was handcrafted and expensive, but the curving, whiplike line was also suitable for mass-produced pieces. Michael Thonet (1796–1871), a German manufacturer, had been making bent and laminated furniture since the 1830s, but with the rise of Art Nouveau and increased industrialization, his factory rapidly expanded to produce a wide range of curvilinear furniture (chairs, tables, rockers) in the new mode. Thonet or "bentwood" furniture is still made, and earlier, signed pieces are eagerly sought out by collectors.

Victorian furniture has begun to attract interest in England but remains largely undiscovered on the Continent, where collectors may purchase well-made mid-nineteenth-century examples at prices barely exceeding those for modern, factory-made furnishings. Victoriana, at present, is a very good buy.

The furnishings of North and South America have, of course, been greatly influenced by European styles. There were English, Dutch, and Spanish settlements in what is now the United States by the early seventeenth century, and furniture in these areas was either brought directly from the homeland or built to resemble European models.

In the United States, New England and most of the Atlantic coast, where the first colonies were established, were dominated by the English. The first furniture they used was in a basically Gothic mode—oak, deeply carved, and rather crude in composition. Experts who have given names to American furniture styles call this the Pilgrim era (1630–1690). Only a few pieces remain from this time, principally chests, cupboards, chairs, and cradles.

By the end of the Pilgrim era Renaissance decorative devices had begun to influence American cabinetmaking; though, just as in England, they were applied to a form and construction that remained essentially Gothic. Large-footed chests and cupboards with open tops for display (known as press cupboards) typify this period. Though still of oak, they are richly carved with floral and geometric Renaissance motifs.

At the very end of the seventeenth century a new influence appeared. The English had absorbed and applied the concepts of the Baroque, and these began to affect the colonies. The American version is termed William and Mary (1690–1720), due to the fact that most furniture made in this country reflects the conservative approach to the Baroque taken in England during the reign of these monarchs. Both form and decoration of American furniture changed greatly during this period. Oak was abandoned for walnut, and various veneers were employed. The chest of drawers, the highboy, the slant-front desk, and the daybed appeared. The use of cushions and caning on chairs became general.

The advent of English Queen Anne furnishings in the period from 1720 to 1750 led to further changes in American style. Colonial furniture development was still lagging behind that of the mother country, but with improved transportation and an expanding middle class eager for new things, it was catching up.

The diluted English version of the Rococo had a profound effect on American cabinetmaking. The bold ball turnings and veneer of the William and Mary era were replaced by graceful, curved elements and wood without inlay or veneer. The cabriole leg made its appearance, and local artisans devised a new tripartite foot called the trifid. By the 1730s mahogany was available, though many cabinetmakers continued to favor abundant native timbers such as walnut, cherry, and maple.

The tall highboy and the chest-on-chest (really a double-decker chest of drawers) were the outstanding pieces of the time. Overstuffed chairs and sofas also appeared. Though examples from furnituremaking centers like Philadelphia and Boston were more elaborate, most American Queen Anne furniture had little carving and relied for its effect on fine wood and graceful lines.

Carving reappeared around 1750, when American workmen began to adopt English Georgian design concepts. So great were the influence and popularity of the Georgian designer Thomas Chippendale that an entire era of American furniture styling is named after him, the Chippendale (1750–1790).

The curving form of the Rococo-Queen Anne style was not entirely abandoned, but it was overlaid with new decorative devices. The upper legs and backs of chairs were richly carved. The ball-and-claw foot replaced the pad and the trifid. Chippendale's straight "Chinese" leg was also adopted for some pieces. But the colonists were not mere copyists. Not only did they subtly alter the Georgian mode to suit their own purposes, but they also devised new forms. At Newport, Rhode Island, the school of cabinetmakers founded by John Goddard and Christopher Townsend created the block front, in which the fronts and drawers of cabinets were shaped so that the centers were recessed and the ends curved outward. Another feature of New England furniture related more to French than English forms was the swelling curve of the bombé-fronted chest of drawers.

Even after the successful conclusion of the War for Independence, American furnituremakers continued to look to England for guidance. The English version of the Classic Revival was reflected in the United States in the designs of the Federal period (1790–1810). The design books of Sheraton and Hepplewhite were reprinted in America, and some well-known native craftsmen, such as John Seymour of Boston and Samuel McIntire of Salem, Massachusetts, created faithful reproductions of English furniture.

American Federal, named in honor of the new republic, is plainer than the English version, but emphasizes the same qualities: delicate compositional balance of verticals and horizontals, fine veneering, and the use of bronze or gilt hardware. Of all the classic decorative devices, the

most popular was the Roman eagle, now adopted as the symbol of the new nation.

The phase of the Classic Revival known in France as Empire and in England as Regency, lingered in the United States, lasting from 1810 to 1840. American Empire designs were somewhat affected by English taste, but with improved travel conditions and an increase in travel abroad, American designers often went directly to France for inspiration.

The two great native interpreters of the style were Duncan Phyfe and Charles Lannuier of New York City. Phyfe's work bridged the gap between Federal and Empire. Lannuier, arriving later on the scene, added an elaborate French quality to the era with rich carving and abundant use of gilt-metal mounts. The early practitioners of American Empire used mahogany, marble, and fine gilt bronze. Their followers, who continued to crank out massive, unattractive pieces for another several decades, employed walnut or walnut veneer and dispensed altogether with metal mountings.

Though the early craftsmen produced fine sofas, decorative side tables, and a variety of gaming and dining surfaces, most later American Empire consists of chairs and chests of drawers. Beds and cabinets are relatively scarce. There is a great deal of nineteenth-century Empire furniture available in the United States at very reasonable prices. Unlike the later Victorian, Empire has never

caught on with collectors, and it remains a fertile field for exploration.

As a country on the move and very open to suggestion, the United States was more receptive than most nations to English Victorian styling. American Victorian (1840–1910) faithfully followed most of the changes in design that took place in English furniture. Moreover, as it rapidly became the world's most industrialized nation, the United States employed factory methods in construction to an even greater extent than England. Sophisticated carving and veneering machinery was developed by the middle of the century, and the great midwestern furniture factories poured out thousands of pieces of virtually machine-made furniture.

But it was also in America that reaction to factory methods was strongest. Though they had little effect in Europe, the concepts of simplicity and function set forth in the English designer Charles Locke Eastlake's book, *Hints on Household Taste*, were taken to heart in North America. Eastlake-style furniture, with its severe lines and unadorned oaken surfaces, was very popular in the United States, as were the creations of William Morris, whose emphasis on Gothic design was instrumental in the rise of the American Mission style. The term "Mission furniture" refers to a fancied resemblance between the simple furniture made in Spanish missions in the western United States during the eighteenth century and the rec-

tangular oak pieces created by such American designers of the late nineteenth century as Gustav Stickley (1857–1942) and Elbert Hubbard (1856–1915). The plain and functional beds, tables, and chairs made by Stickley and Hubbard have become extremely popular with American collectors in recent years, and signed Mission furniture brings very high prices, though it is often less than fifty years old.

Other interesting American Victorian furnishings include horn furniture such as chairs with backs, sides, arms, and legs made from buffalo or cattle horns. These pieces were popularized by President Theodore Roosevelt, and many examples were manufactured by Tiffany and Company. Bamboo furnishings, inspired by turn-of-the-century Chinese and Japanese imports, are also popular. One may safely say however, that *all* American Victorian furniture, from fine early carved rosewood to cheap factory-made golden oak, is in great demand among Ameri-

can collectors. It is far and away the most popular and the most available of all early American furniture.

While English influence was important, other factors also affected the development of American furniture. Seventeenth- and early-eighteenth-century New York furniture was influenced by Dutch Baroque design, reflecting Holland's brief domination of New York City and the Hudson Valley during the 1600s. Spain controlled large areas of the American Southwest until the middle of the nineteenth century, and the heavy carving, massive ironwork, and rather crude forms characteristic of Spanish colonial styles lingered in that area until the end of the century. Likewise, French settlements at New Orleans and other areas on the Mississippi drew French furniture-makers who worked in the Rococo manner of Louis XV. American purchase of the French-held areas in 1803 did not end these influences, and traces of them still remain in the houses and furnishings of New Orleans.

Canada, too, had its importations. The bitter struggle between England and France for that section of North America left a nation divided stylistically as well as politically. In French Canada—Quebec and other areas under French control until the late eighteenth century—the prevalent style was that of the French provinces. Cupboards with diamond-point panels in the early Baroque style of Louis XIII were made in Canada as late as the 1800s, just as they were in rural areas of France, where the older modes had remained frozen in time while city cabinetmakers created new modes. More sophisticated regions and large cities such as Montreal had designers who followed all of the French styles right down through the Empire period.

English-speaking areas, on the other hand, adopted the forms of their motherland, particularly after the American Revolution, when many Loyalist cabinetmakers fled across the border. High-quality Queen Anne, Chippendale, and Classic Revival furniture may still be found in the older towns of British Canada.

As in the United States, Canadian style was affected by a cultural lag. New forms were accepted reluctantly, particularly in rural areas where country types related to those of Europe held sway for many years, and styles were often as much as fifty years behind those prevailing in Europe. Even when accepted, new forms were simplified and generally made from native woods (with the exception of the ubiquitous imported mahogany).

The pre-Columbian peoples of South America used little furniture, and little of what they did use has survived. Stone tables and chairs have been found in Central and South America, but these are not of much interest to the collector. They are massive and crude, bearing little resemblance to the sophisticated metalwork and textile design these cultures produced.

Spanish and Portuguese colonists introduced their own European styles in the seventeenth century. The furniture, which is characterized by an extravagant Baroque style with excessive and sometimes incoherent ornamentation, is collectively termed Spanish Colonial. Native woods were employed, carving was heavy, and the Iberian penchant for use of ironwork was quite evident. Though later modes were introduced, the Baroque has continued into this century as the favorite South American style.

Though more forms exist in Europe and the Americas, China, as one of the world's most ancient cultures, has long been a center of furniture design. A few forms (chairs, beds, tables, and cupboards) were developed before or soon after the advent of the Christian era, and these have been maintained with little modification for hundreds of years. There are, accordingly, no significant periodic stylistic developments such as one finds in Europe and North America. Moreover, practically all extant specimens date from the Ming (1368–1644) and Ching (1644–1912) dynasty periods, though it is evident from drawings and paintings and from clay and iron miniatures found in tombs that a great deal of furniture did exist before the fourteenth century.

There are really two types of Chinese furniture, each related to a mode of living. In the temperate North the much older style prevailed. There, people lived (and in some cases still do live) at floor level, spending much of their time on an elevated, heated, and mat-covered platform known as a *kang*. Chairs were not used in this area, and tables and cupboards were customarily low to accommodate people who squatted or reclined most of the time. So great was the *kang's* influence on furnishings that the lower northern types have come to be known as *kang* pieces.

In the warmer South, even before 1000 A.D., the *kang*

**Opposite: Pair of Chinese clothes
cupboards, Ming dynasty (1368–1644). These
cupboards, made of *chang mu* wood, are
decorated with carved fretwork and brass fittings.
Below left: Siamese gilt and lacquered wood
cabinet, 17th–18th century. The upper doors are
ornamented with a Buddhist allegorical
scene in lacquer; the base is
carved. Below right: Chinese armchair, *c.* 1700.
This chair, of the type known as a *hua li*,
reflects the purity of line western students of
Chinese furniture find so appealing.**

had become a bed and then a couch: chairs, which had appeared in the second century as a complement to the ancient low stool, occupied space made available by the disappearance of the platform and the enlargement of the traditional living area. Tables became higher as the family moved from floor to seat level. Small square or rectangular tables for writing or use as light stands were employed, but the most important piece of this sort was the large round dining table. The Chinese still favor such tables, as they facilitate eating or serving from a common bowl or bowls placed in the center of the piece.

The chair appears to have been introduced into China by Indians or westerners, as indicated by its name, *hu ch'uang*, or "barbarian couch." The earliest examples are little more than square stools with backs; but from the Ming period on one finds armchairs, high-backed wing chairs, and many different side chairs. Various hardwoods are employed, as well as bamboo.

As life moved from the platform to the floor, chests and cupboards became higher and took new shapes, such as

the large standing cupboard or armoire, which both by its size and decoration and by its placement in the room is judged the most important piece of Chinese furniture. Such armoires are typically made in pairs and may have matching hatboxes or smaller companion chests made and decorated in the same manner. Another southern development was the desk, though it appears that this piece was inspired largely by European examples introduced during the seventeenth and eighteenth centuries.

Contrary to popular belief, most Chinese furniture is not made of teak, nor is it lacquered. Most is made of camphor or of highly polished hardwoods such as rosewood or mahogany. Lines are severe and classical. Inlay, though found, does not usually appear on the best pieces.

Japanese furniture is closely related to that of China, though far less variety is found. Japanese styles were largely fixed through the adoption between the seventh and tenth centuries of Chinese Tang dynasty furnishings. Since China at this time was still in the *kang* period, such pieces were low and limited in type.

Those antique Japanese tables that are found are low in stature and made of lacquered or highly polished wood. Most cupboards are built into walls. They range from narrow series of drawers to combinations of drawers and hanging cupboards for clothing that may cover an entire wall. There are few chairs other than the folding type used by military officers in the field. Early chests, based on Tang models, were long and low and of highly polished hardwood. During the seventeenth century these were supplemented by portable chests called *tansu*. Since these were intended for travel, they often have handles and are brass- or ironbound. They may also be decorated with lacquerwork, carving, or inlay.

Since the 1880s large quantities of Chinese furniture, particularly chests and cupboards, have been exported

64

from Canton and Hong Kong. Though often inferior in quality and workmanship to the furnishings made for domestic use, these pieces are of interest to foreign collectors. In general, the earlier pieces are the better ones, and these should not be confused with the great quantity of teak and camphor furniture that has been made since the 1950s. Much of this later furniture is made of unseasoned wood and is soon reduced to kindling in the steam-heated western home.

Korean furniture forms closely follow those of China, though there are variations both in workmanship and decoration. Like the Japanese, the Koreans were very fond of chests, and the carved decoration on these may be of high quality. As with Chinese and Japanese examples, most decorative motifs are based on Buddhist religious symbols and floral abstractions. Unfortunately, the almost constant violence and disruption that have marked Korea's history have left us few examples of early furniture, and even eighteenth- and nineteenth-century pieces are hard to come by.

Furniture was, of course, also produced in other areas of Asia. Indeed, as mentioned, the chair may have come to China from India; and the latter country, along with Thailand, has long been known for its elaborately decorated small chests and tables.

The climate and the life styles of the people of the Pacific islands, on the other hand, militate against use of much furniture. In a tropical area plagued by typhoons, there is little incentive to construct large furnishings, and only small and rudimentary forms are found. Traditionally, the only seating furniture was the chief's stool, and its function was more ceremonial than practical, serving to elevate the ruler above his subjects. In keeping with its role, the chief's stool is usually elaborately carved or painted and is generally used only on state occasions.

In the Cook Islands area rough plank beds are found, but these may reflect European influence; most Polynesians use a mat and a wooden headrest for sleeping. These headrests are designed to support the nape of the neck rather than to cushion the head. As this is also the style of Chinese and Japanese pillows, it reinforces the theory that the settlers of these islands originally came from Asia.

Even in the great expanse of Africa one does not find much in the way of indigenous furnishings. Prior to the coming of the whites, stools were the only seating accommodation. There were a few small wooden traveling chests and crude tables. As in Polynesia, stools were generally associated with the nobility, so carved and painted decoration was the rule.

Once the Europeans had established themselves, white and native craftsmen produced colonial furniture modeled on European forms. In western Africa, black craftsmen built armchairs in crude simulation of the Baroque style for their kings, while somewhat more sophisticated examples of Dutch-influenced furnishings were produced in the region of Cape Town, South Africa. In Kenya and other portions of eastern Africa, English Victorian furniture was manufactured, usually by English craftsmen. French and German furniture styles influenced construction in areas colonized by those nations, but none of these furnishings ever reached the artistic quality attained by the black African decorative arts.

Much of the appeal inherent in the collecting of antique furniture relates to its utilitarian quality. It was once used by people like us; and, in most cases, we can also use it. As a consequence, more and more collectors are not merely acquiring but are actually utilizing the old furniture of their homelands. They are, in a very real sense, living with history.

3

3
Gold and Silver

Preceding pp.: English silver brazier,
1735–1739. This serving dish was created by
Charles Frederick Kandler of London, a
well-known 18th-century silversmith. It is in
the late Rococo style. Above: Russian
silver beaker, 18th century. Engraved decoration
depicts the Imperial eagle of czarist Russia.

People have always been attracted by the variety and beauty of the precious metals, and with the exception of remote and primitive areas such as the Pacific islands, gold- and silverworking have been long-established crafts in all parts of the world. The European guild system, which strictly governed not only the selection and training of gold- and silversmiths but also the type and quality of the objects they made, can be traced to the Middle Ages. But controls in this area are far older. They were part of the laws of ancient Persia, and an Egyptian goldsmith's weight exists that bears the mark of a monarch who ruled in the fourth millennium before Christ.

These regulations were necessitated in part by the scarcity of the ores. Since gold and silver are rare metals as well as beautiful and easily worked, they have long been the prerogative of the rich and the royal, and in many societies their ownership and use have been restricted by law or tradition to the upper classes. In some areas, in fact, and particularly with gold, the metal itself became an element of the religious and political structure. This was especially true in Africa and in the sun-worshiping nations of South America.

The unique quality of gold and silver, the one that sets them apart from nearly all other materials of which antiques are made, is the fact that they have great value even in an unworked state. Objects made of these metals have suffered greatly because of this characteristic. In time of war or need it is far easier to sell or transport a block of gold or a silver coin than it is a tea service or a platter, and vast quantities of gold and silver artifacts have been melted down and effectively destroyed under such circumstances. Nevertheless, enough remains to provide us with substantial insight into the working methods of ancient craftsmen.

Interestingly, very little seems new in the art of shaping and decorating the precious metals. Since earliest times smiths have known how to hammer and mold them. Since both gold and silver are extremely soft and malleable, wrought or raised pieces can be created by hammering a sheet of metal into shape, usually over a wooden form. Since both melt at a relatively low temperature, they can be cast in molds as well.

Nor does decoration vary greatly. From Colombia to Syria to England one finds the same basic decorative techniques. These are chiefly piercing, or creating patterns by cutting holes through the metal; repoussé, or embossing designs by hammering from the interior of a hollow piece; chasing, or hammering designs into the object from the surface; and engraving, in which the metal skin is cut or scraped away to create the design.

These methods of shaping and decorating gold and silver have been employed throughout the world for thousands of years. In the nineteenth century, western craftsmen added to them. They developed the technique of spinning, whereby a sheet of silver or gold was worked into shape by being turned on a lathe; and, more important, they created Sheffield and electroplate silver. The former is a metal "sandwich" consisting of a sheet of copper overlaid on each side with a thin sheet of silver and bound together by being run through giant roller presses. English scientists improved on Sheffield silver by developing electroplating, a chemical process by which silver in solution is made to adhere to a base metal such as copper or Britannia metal (an alloy of tin, antimony, and copper). Since much of the collectible silver available today is Sheffield or electroplate, these techniques are of great importance to the antiquarian.

The development of Sheffield and electroplate silver brings to light some of the problems inherent in the working of gold and silver. First, since the ores are rare and valuable, it has long been the smith's dream to dilute them with less expensive metals so as to maintain the feel and appearance of the unalloyed metal while actually using less of it. Second, both gold and silver are too soft in their natural state to be of much use. They can be worked, but the resultant objects are easily dented or scratched. The addition of another metal such as copper greatly increases the hardness of the precious ores.

The use of alloys is essential in the working of gold and silver, but it can lead to abuse. To the greedy or impecunious craftsman, if a little base metal is a good thing, then a whole lot is even better. Accordingly, from the earliest times and in nearly all societies, rigid standards of purity have been imposed. In the western world the purity of gold is measured in karats. Twenty-four-karat gold is pure, completely unalloyed; 18-karat gold is composed of 18 parts gold and 6 parts base metal. Silver is dealt with in a somewhat different manner. Before 1800, national coinage in England and North America was required to be 900 parts silver, 100 parts alloy. Silver meeting this standard was termed "coin silver." After 1800, however, most silver utensils (except spoons) were made not of coin but of sterling, which is 925 parts silver to 75 parts alloy. This difference reflects government efforts to prevent the melting down of coins to make silverware. If the coinage was below the sterling standard it would be less likely to end up on the table instead of in the pocket.

As the more valuable ore and the one traditionally associated with royalty, gold has often received the finer workmanship. Magnificent gold utensils and jewelry were manufactured in ancient Egypt, Sumeria, Persia, Greece, and Rome. The few objects that have survived, mostly from burial sites, attest to remarkable taste and sophisticated techniques, including casting, raising, and various decorative procedures.

Gold was clearly of great importance to the dynasties of Europe and the Near East, but nowhere was it more honored than in South America, where pre-Columbian sun-worshiping societies stored the metal as a religious act. The Indians of Ecuador, Peru, Mexico, Costa Rica, Colombia, and Panama worked both gold and silver, but most of their finer pieces were in gold.

Craftsmen in what is now Colombia displayed distinct regional styles and employed a sculptural approach with perfectly balanced masses and volumes. They were the first in the Americas to employ soldering and casting, and they achieved fine representations of human and animal forms. The Mixtecs of Mexico were known for their cast and hammered work, while the thirteenth-century Chimu of Peru developed sophisticated decorative techniques including gilding, beading, and embossing.

The Chimu and Mixtecs also worked in silver, the latter creating grotesque and powerful funeral or mummy masks. Best known of the South American silversmiths, though, are the Incas, who made engraved silver dishes and beakers in the form of human heads.

After the destruction of the pre-Columbian cultures by Spanish and Portuguese colonizers, nearly all the native gold and silver vessels were melted down for shipment to Europe as bullion. The local craftsmen who were not slain worked for their conquerors in European styles, though they were severely limited by a decree of Philip II forbidding Indians to own or work precious metals. Nevertheless, certain colonial work is known, chiefly crosses and candlesticks from Mexico and brandy casks from Bolivia. Most eighteenth- and nineteenth-century South American gold and silver objects, however, were made by transplanted European craftsmen, who closely followed the fashions of the mother country in style and technique.

In Africa, too, dynasties were built on gold. While silver

Colombian gold pendant in the form of a
figure with a large headdress, Sierra Nevada area,
13th–14th century. Colombian goldsmiths
were masters of casting and filigree work, often
assembling even small pieces like
this one from components that were carefully
soldered together. This piece, in the
Tairona style, is an effigy figure that no
doubt served a religious purpose.

was seldom used south of the Sahara, the refining and working of gold was a highly developed art, particularly among the Ashanti people of what is now southern Ghana.

For the Ashanti gold was a symbol of life and power and the color of the king. Accordingly, only royalty could work the metal, and goldsmiths' guilds were appendages of the royal court. (Membership in the guilds was hereditary: goldsmiths passed on their craft and their tools to their sons.) So closely, in fact, was gold associated with the Ashanti belief in a divine kingship that the soul of the tribe was believed to be enshrined in a golden stool owned by the *Omahene*, or king.

Despite the Ashanti's obsession with the yellow ore, relatively few forms (compared with European and American wares) were made from it. There are umbrella finials, cups and bowls, and *kudu*, golden boxes believed to contain the souls of departed ancestors. Pendants, either cast or of fine filigree work, were also popular, and

a few magnificent ritual masks are known. Though much of this work was destroyed during colonization and in tribal wars, a sufficient quantity remains to tell us that the Africans were among the world's greatest goldsmiths. Eighteenth- and nineteenth-century African gold, most of it Ashanti, is still available and is of great interest to collectors.

As with most other antiques, though, the greatest variety and quantity of gold and silver artifacts is found in Europe and North America. The dominant ancient centers of gold- and silversmithing were Egypt, the Near East, and Greece and Rome, but one can hardly consider the rare artifacts of these civilizations collectible antiques. Therefore, our focus will be on European gold and silver of later periods.

As with other arts, much craftsmanship in precious metals was lost during the Dark Ages following the collapse of the Roman Empire. A great many skills survived, however, and the few existing medieval examples show

a high quality of workmanship and design—one quite superior to that evidenced, for example, in furniture of the same period. These rare pieces of gold and silver, whatever their local origin, have something in common—a style. That is, they reflect a consistent point of view as to design, which in turn indicates the existence of a well-organized and relatively cosmopolitan work force.

This work force was the guild, a close-knit, hierarchical organization of highly trained craftsmen. The origins of the guilds are lost in antiquity, but by the Middle Ages they were well established in Europe. Since it was in the interests of the ruling class to assure that precious metals were unadulterated and properly crafted, the guilds early came under the royal thumb. They existed by governmental sufferance, and governmental regulations largely dictated their form.

Since it was vital that precious ores be handled by honest and capable workmen, a period of apprenticeship, usually seven years, was prescribed. During this period the would-be craftsman was trained and observed to see if he was both apt and true. At the end of this time, and often following the making of a test or "graduation" piece to be approved by his teachers, the apprentice advanced to the rank of journeyman. He was given a suit of clothes and a set of tools and was free to work in his craft for a wage. Then, following a further period of training, he might attain the status of master craftsman, entitling him to set up on his own.

The importance of the apprentice system cannot be underestimated. Since most apprentices copied the work of their masters, innovations in the craft tended to be absorbed and refined by guild masters and then perpetuated by those whom they trained.

The first of the great stylistic periods was the Gothic, which held sway during the thirteenth to fifteenth cen-

and then filling these frames with enamel. The latter technique is known as cloisonné.

Much silver was gilded at this time. A solution of gold and mercury was applied to a piece of silver and then heated until the mercury evaporated, leaving a film of gold over the silver. If the object was only partly covered with gold it was said to be "parcel" gilded. Gilding was very popular in the Gothic era not only because a gilded piece looked "richer" but also because gold, unlike silver, does not tarnish and is immune to the destructive effects of salt. The latter quality was particularly significant in the late Middle Ages because of the ceremonial importance of the "master salt," the centerpiece of every upper-class dining table. Since salt was vital both as a flavoring and as a preservative, and since it was expensive and hard to obtain, it was a valuable item—so valuable, in fact, that status at the table was traditionally defined by where one sat in relation to the master salt. Those of high degree or in special favor with the master of the house sat above the salt, all others sat below. Given its social significance, it would hardly do for a householder to have a dingy or corroded salt cellar.

Mercury gilding was an effective decorative device. It was, however, also rather dangerous for the workmen who used it. Many gilders suffered a painful and prolonged death from poisoning caused by inhaling fumes from the evaporating mercury. Yet it was not until the introduction of electrolysis in the mid-nineteenth century that this technique was abandoned.

Most of the important Gothic gold and silver vessels still extant come from the colder northern European countries such as Germany, England, and Scandinavia. The style lingered there long after the introduction of newer styles from other areas.

Italy, remaining under the sway of its classical heritage,

turies. Design at this time was largely dictated by architecture, for during the period when the great churches of northern Europe were being constructed, all other craftsmen tended to imitate the decorative patterns employed by stonemasons. Spiky fretwork, pinnacles, rigid leaf patterns, and cusping and lobing are characteristic of the work of this era.

Gothic gold and silver tends to be massive and heavily decorated. Precious or semiprecious stones are frequently set into the metal—pearls, garnets, and emeralds appear to have been among the more popular gems. Other forms of embellishment were also used. Metals might be enameled, either by setting colors into an area where the surface had been cut away (a process known as champlevé) or by soldering wires to the surface in various patterns

1

2

3

never really took to the Gothic. And it was in Italy, of course, that the next great style was born. In the early fifteenth century goldsmiths in Florence began to develop their own manner, a mixture of local tradition and new eastern motifs. Like their northern counterparts, the Italians drew heavily on architecture for inspiration, in this case the surviving buildings of ancient Greece and Rome. The shapes of gold and silver vessels reflected the columns, pilasters, and friezes of antiquity. From wall paintings found on newly excavated Roman buildings, artisans adapted the curly forms of vines and acanthus leaves, the classic lines of ancient urns, and the cheerful grotesquery of satyrs, and translated them into decorative patterns.

Gold and silver objects of this period, such as ewers, vases, and large plates, are, accordingly, architectural and rectilinear in nature. Decoration tends to be set off in panels or reserves with various heraldic motifs, bulbous shapes, and relatively simple ornamentation. The sculptural effects were achieved chiefly by casting, at which Italian workmen were adept. Embossed decoration was also popular.

Florence led the way, for Italy and the world, and it was here that gold- and silversmiths emerged as individuals. Prior to the Renaissance anonymity was the rule, and little work could be associated with individual craftsmen. During the Renaissance, though, the crafters of precious metals declared themselves (or were declared by royal patrons) to be artists. Thus began the tradition of signed or otherwise identifiable ware, a custom that has continued to the present.

The greatest of all known Florentine goldsmiths, and one of the foremost of all times, was Benvenuto Cellini (1500–1571). He wrote several texts on the subject and made a magnificent gold-and-enamel salt cellar for François I of France.

4

The French had discovered Renaissance metalwork during military campaigns near Naples, and it was not long before their nobility were employing Cellini and other Italian artisans to design their gold and silver vessels. Because of this direct and continuing influence, French metalware of the Renaissance period closely follows Italian fashions.

German decoration was far more elaborate than Italian and French. Naturalistic motifs were favored. A cup might take the form of a columbine or a knotty tree trunk. Ceremonial drinking vessels owned by various craft or occupational organizations would be shaped to suit the honored group. The fishmongers' guild, for example, would drink from fish-shaped beakers, and a tankard in the form of a cow's head would grace the butchers' table. The Germans also pioneered in the use of materials generally not associated with precious metals. They used coconuts and nautilus shells for the bowls of silver-bound cups, for example, and a salt cellar might be made of an ostrich egg mounted on a golden stand. They also employed large quantities of gemstones. Ceremonial vessels might be entirely encrusted with jewels, a Gothic custom that remained a powerful influence on Germanic taste.

During the period when they were blessed with a steady flow of rare ore from their South American colonies, Spain and Portugal created some of the finest Renaissance metalwork. Sixteenth-century Spanish gold- and silverware was primarily ecclesiastical, and the greatest efforts were often lavished on such things as 6-foot-high (1.8-m) silver monstrances, or custodia (vessels that held holy relics), which were carried in religious processions. The greatest Spanish silversmith of the period was Juan Arfe (1535–1603), who specialized in making custodia.

English gold- and silverwork of the Renaissance period was much influenced by German forms. Henry VIII was

very conscious of Italian styles and was influential in eliminating the final vestiges of English Gothic. At first he imported Italian workmen, but after his break with the Roman church he replaced them with Germans, including the painter Hans Holbein the Younger, who was also a silver designer. English silver of this period was often made by Germans or in accordance with German pattern books and may be difficult to distinguish from German pieces. Like their teachers, the English favored pieces mounted on unusual materials such as stoneware, rock crystal, or coconut.

It was in England that Crown and guild supervision of gold- and silverwork reached its greatest development. There was an English goldsmiths' guild as early as 1180, and a royal charter was granted to the Guild of London Goldsmiths in 1327. By the sixteenth century London's Goldsmiths' Hall was the site of an elaborate testing process for determining the quality of precious metals.

As early as 1300, Edward I had ordered that gold be "of the touch of Paris" and silver of "esterling allay." It became the duty of the Wardens of Goldsmiths' Hall to determine if precious metals met these standards.

Remarkably proficient, the wardens could determine the silver content of an alloy simply by rubbing the metal on a touchstone and comparing the color of the mark with that of an unalloyed touch. Gold and silver objects that passed the test were stamped with codes adopted by the Hall to indicate their quality (hence the term "hallmark"). Hallmarks have changed over the years, and by referring to books on the subject, one can determine the date and place of manufacture of a given piece from its hallmark. Though these marks have been used in other countries, nowhere else has the system been so complete or remained in operation as long as it has in England. Even today, a piece of silver or gold containing too much alloy is broken up and returned, unmarked, to its maker.

In the late seventeenth century the Dutch, who had initially followed Germanic forms and pattern books, came to the fore as designers and craftsmen. Such famous smiths as the Van Vianems popularized a more florid version of Italian Renaissance style characterized by elaborately embossed genre scenes and sinuous curves. Dutch engraving, particularly of floral patterns featuring the ubiquitous tulip, was also of high quality.

In some respects these Dutch innovations heralded a new style, the Baroque. The first signs of change, however, had come in Italy during the Counter Reformation. Seeking to regain lost patronage, the Catholic church built or rebuilt cathedrals in a dazzling style emphasizing bold curves and florid three-dimensional details that were in sharp contrast to the more austere taste of the Italian Renaissance. The architectural developments were soon mirrored in the other arts, including precious metalwork, and the changes traveled swiftly to other lands.

In France, Jean Berain, Louis XIV's court designer, modified Italian gold and silver designs to emphasize complex composition and sharp contrasts in light and color. Using Berain's designs, the royal Gobelin factory at Paris produced a vast array of plate for the palace at Versailles. Much of this, regrettably, was later melted down.

When Charles II returned to England after exile in Holland he brought with him examples of Dutch Baroque ware, decorated with elaborate floral ornaments and heavy embossing. Much of this new Dutch ware also bore the influence of the East. Trade with the Orient had greatly increased, and both shape and decoration were affected thereby. There were entirely new pieces (new to the West, that is) such as teapots and tea caddies, or canisters. There was also chinoiserie ornamentation, adapted from Oriental lacquerware, textiles, and porcelain and modified to suit the needs of western metalsmiths.

Despite its use of eastern elements, Dutch Baroque metalware, like its English and German counterparts, was still taking much from France, for French influence was reaching its zenith during this period. French taste spread as a result of persecution of the Huguenots. Fleeing religious prejudice, many French Protestants emigrated to England and Germany, bringing a variety of skills including metalsmithing. It was they who carried to England, where embossing had been the chief form of decoration, the techniques of casting and piercing.

Extreme richness of ornamentation eventually becomes tiresome, and the Baroque was gradually transformed into a less ornate style, the Rococo. Here again, the French led the way. In reaction to the ponderous grandeur of the prior reign, French designers of the Louis XV period emphasized soft borders and natural forms. Symmetry was abandoned in favor of swirling leaves and organic *rocaille* (rockwork) shapes. A major influence in the development of the French Rococo was Juste-Aurèle Meissonier (1695–1750), a renowned silversmith of the period. Meissonier's designs and those of Thomas Germain (1673–1748), another well-known metalworker, were adopted not only in France but as far away as Russia and Portugal.

The Rococo spread quickly throughout Europe, being particularly popular in Bavaria and England. In the latter country, the embossing and casting favored in the prior period were now combined with chasing, engraving, piercing, and cut work to achieve wild and even bizarre decorative effects. Scotland and Ireland also followed England's lead in embracing the Rococo, though they had their own specialties: the dish ring (a type of trivet) in Ireland and the lovely heart-shaped brooches of Scotland. Although pear-shaped forms, especially noticeable in canisters, teapots, and coffeepots, were characteristic of the style, form was really secondary to ornament in the Rococo. Outlines were determined by the juxtaposition of decorative motifs. As a result, a number of elements, each attractive in itself, might in combination become distorted and exaggerated.

Again, it was only a matter of time before reaction set in. By the middle of the eighteenth century a longing for simplicity once more asserted itself. The search for classic elegance and restraint was initially prompted by the ex-

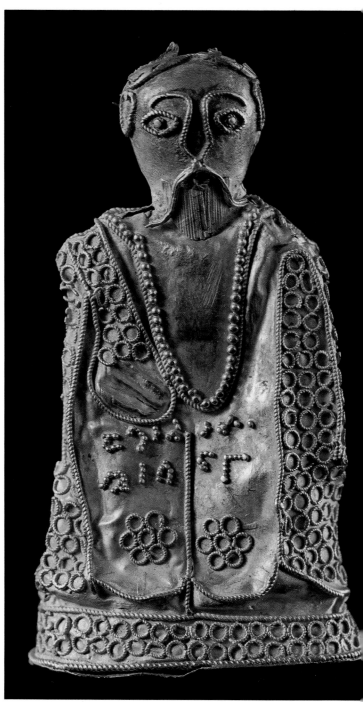

cavation of the ancient Roman city of Herculaneum. Digging here, which began in the 1730s, was followed in 1755 by the discovery of Pompeii. Both towns had been buried by the eruption of Mt. Vesuvius in 79 A.D.; within them, sealed beneath a protective mantle—ash in the case of Herculaneum and lava at Pompeii—lay the artistic heritage of Greece and Rome. Wall paintings, tilework, metalware, and pottery all were there.

European designers flocked to the sites, and from their discoveries a new classicism (appropriately termed the Neoclassic) was born—or reborn, perhaps, for Europe had never really abandoned the Renaissance-inspired study of Greece and Rome.

As the Neoclassic spread throughout Europe, gold and silver forms were modeled on the urns, vases, and bowls being dug up, as well as on the architecture being uncovered. Emphasis was, once more, on design, structure, and perfect proportions. Simple curves and unbroken outlines replaced the lush construction of the Rococo.

Greek and Roman columns became candlesticks. From the classical urn emerged sauce bowls, teapots, and chocolate pots. Casting and embossing were deemphasized in favor of decoration in low relief, often achieved by stamping thin metal between dies or cutting it into attractive openwork patterns. Colored glass fillers were frequently employed with openwork. As in the early Renaissance, classical motifs such as fluting, beading, oval medallions, floral swags, and acanthus leaves were the decorations of choice.

The arrival of the Neoclassic period in gold and silver design coincided to some extent with another extremely important event, the development of Sheffield silver, or Sheffield plate (the term "plate" refers to silver flatware in general). In 1742 Thomas Boulsover, a cutler working in Sheffield, England, a town long famous for its high-quality steel and silver, accidentally discovered that silver would adhere to copper if heated. Within a few years a technique had been developed whereby a slab of copper between two slabs of silver was placed in an oven until the silver began to melt. The material was then removed and allowed to cool before being run through large roller presses, which reduced it to the desired thickness.

Sheffield silver was an immediate hit with the European middle class, for it looked and could be decorated like sterling but, because of its lower silver content, was much less expensive. Since it came into favor at the beginning of the Neoclassic period, much Sheffield is found in this form.

At first most Sheffield was unmarked, but it was not long before manufacturers began using hallmarks that looked very much like those found on sterling. This presented a serious threat to English silver manufacturers, for Sheffield was not just a cheap substitute for silver—it was well made and, indeed, could be mistaken for sterling. In 1773 the silversmiths obtained a court order preventing Sheffield manufacturers from employing deceptive marks. When this ban was lifted, in 1784, it was with the understanding that all Sheffield would bear the name of its maker and the word "Sheffield" or some other distinguishing mark. As a result, most Sheffield from the period 1784 to approximately 1850 is clearly marked.

Sheffield silver is most collectible today. It was made in most of the forms one finds in sterling during the Neoclassic and the following early Victorian period, and it is both attractive and relatively inexpensive.

Some of the finest Neoclassic silver and gold objects were made in England, where Robert Adam, an architect and designer, worked directly from ancient examples to derive his own interpretations of classic themes. His designs were executed by many English smiths, including

Hester Bateman and Mary Makemeid, two of the very few women silver producers. Frequently seen examples of English Neoclassic silver are baskets, mustardpots, and covered sugar bowls, all slim and elegant and decorated with delicate engraving.

Continental Neoclassic gold and silver tended to be more elaborate than that produced in England. For the most part, the same general forms—serving dishes, platters, tea and coffee services—were produced; but whereas English decoration was confined almost entirely to engraving, European examples employed piercing, applied and cast decoration, and engraving, often all on the same piece.

Perhaps the most popular and collectible European Neoclassic pieces are the small silver and gold boxes that were made in France and Russia. These became the rage among the nobility and the wealthy during the late eighteenth century, and smiths vied to produce the most precious and exotic examples. Some boxes were encrusted with precious gems, others were made partially of tortoiseshell or mother-of-pearl, and still others bore elaborate enameled pictures, a technique especially popular in Russia.

The Neoclassic revival lasted well into the nineteenth century, but its form changed over time. The delicacy and slender elegance of the late eighteenth century gradually gave way to monumental forms and an emphasis on exact copies of ancient treasures. This latter phase, which coincided with the Empire period in furnituremaking, saw the production, particularly in France, of pieces that were massive and sculptural—and often boring as well. French decoration, like English, relied heavily on motifs taken from ancient Greek and Roman examples. The French added something more, however. Following their conquest of Egypt they employed Egyptian decorative devices, such as the lotus.

Opposite: Chinese silver ball,
Sung dynasty (960–1279). The exact purpose
of this piece is unknown, but later
objects similar to this one were used as
hand warmers, incense burners, and
decorations. Below: Japanese cast and raised
gold pouch ornament, 19th century.
Only 3½ inches (9 cm) long, piece depicts six
of the seven Japanese gods of
happiness carousing at a festive table.

By the 1830s the creative drive of the Neoclassic was largely spent, and gold- and silverware manufacture began to be influenced by the same eclecticism that was affecting furnituremaking. Instead of creating new, unified styles as they had done in the past, smiths simply reused elements of old ones—Baroque, Gothic, or whatever. This period, the Victorian, lasted from the 1830s to about 1910.

Most Victorian gold and silver was characterized by extravagant ornamentation, and most was factory-made rather than handmade. The introduction of Sheffield silver and the employment, as early as the 1780s, of mechanical cutting and stamping devices had foreshadowed the demise of the individual silversmith; the development of electroplating greatly accelerated that demise. In the late 1830s John Wright, a Birmingham surgeon, discovered that by passing an electric current through a solution containing cyanide of silver, it was possible to deposit an even coat of silver on a copper bar. Wright's process was purchased and patented in 1840 by the Birmingham silversmith George Elkington.

Electroplating revolutionized the silver industry. More durable than silver, cheaper than Sheffield, electroplate ware was available to all but the very poor. Elkington and his successors, like the well-known James Dixon and Sons of Sheffield, produced hundreds of different items in the new plate, including tea and coffee sets, salts, canisters, serving dishes, and platters. By the 1870s English and American electroplate silver was being shipped throughout the western world, effectively putting an end to most Sheffield and sterling production.

Electroplate is now something of a rage among collectors. For years it was ignored, partly out of snobbery, partly because the design was sometimes poor, but modern enthusiasts have come to recognize that it is the best buy in nineteenth-century silver still available. Vast quantities exist (mostly from the period 1850 to 1920), nearly all of which bear manufacturer's marks, and prices remain low. Much of the ware, it is true, is found in a worn condition with the copper or Britannia-metal base showing through in spots, but collectors have discovered that such pieces can be resilvered at a fraction of what a comparable modern example would cost.

The criticism most often leveled at electroplate, and Victorian gold and silver in general, is that it tends to be overornamented and without discernible style. That is certainly true of some ware. The employment of elements from several stylistic periods in a single piece led to some odd results. On the other hand, when Victorian silver manufacturers found a unified style, their achievements rivaled those of prior periods. Such was the case with Art Nouveau. At the close of the nineteenth century, French and English designers, influenced by Rococo form and decoration, developed a style characterized by elongated proportions and swirling, elegant lines. Lighter and more sophisticated than other Victorian ware and decorated with appealing motifs associated with natural elements such as leaves and tree trunks, Art Nouveau gold and silver were popular in their period (1890–1915) and are undergoing an extensive revival today. French, English, and German Art Nouveau precious metalwares are all in demand.

Craftsmanship in the precious metals developed somewhat differently in North America than in Europe. There were gold- and silversmiths in the colonies as early as the seventeenth century, but their work was sharply limited by lack of native raw materials. It was not until the great western strikes of the mid-nineteenth century that North America had its own source of ore. Before that time gold and silver had to be imported at high cost or obtained by the melting down of older ware or coins.

The craft system worked differently as well. The earliest smiths were immigrants, but gradually a class of native artisans grew up. These men served an apprenticeship just as they might have in Europe, but not under the supervision of a king or guild master. In the United States, especially, the government took a "hands-off" attitude toward the crafts, a position consistent with new concepts of personal liberty.

In the United States there were never true guilds, and hallmarking, while practiced, was done only to identify ware as to silver content and maker (or perhaps to fool the buyer into thinking he or she was purchasing preferred English silver). The only government attempt to control the alloy content of precious metals was the establishment of an assay office in Baltimore from 1814 to 1830. For the most part, quality was controlled by peer pressure and public opinion.

Stylistically, American silver and gold follow European forms and periods, usually with a few years' cultural lag. English interpretations of Baroque, Rococo, and Neoclassic are most common, though Dutch Baroque had a strong early influence in New York City, and craftsmen of other nationalities also made their mark. Forms were generally less complex and less ornamental than their European counterparts, and gold was less used—as the metal traditionally associated with royalty, it was not popular in a republic. Besides, few could afford to own it prior to the Victorian era.

Since most American silversmiths marked their wares with their name or an identifying cipher, we have been able to learn quite a bit about the more prominent craftsmen. Among these, of course, was Paul Revere of Boston, whose exploits in the War for Independence have made his name a byword in American history. Revere did a variety of things, including making bells, but he was primarily a silversmith, and a very good one. Other well-known eighteenth-century figures in the trade were John Burt, Jacob Hurd, and John Coney, also of Boston; Myer Myers of New York; and Philip Syng of Philadelphia. Workers from many other areas have also been identified.

Though they might have been influenced by European styles, most American silversmiths were not content to be slavish copyists, and in the late nineteenth century they were instrumental in developing the Art Nouveau mode. True, this fashion arose concurrently in Europe, but American designers proved at least as innovative. Tiffany and Company of New York is well known for the marvelous gold and silver objects its designers created at the turn of the century. By 1890 Tiffany was the largest silversmith in the world and held appointments to do work for more than twenty heads of state, including Queen Victoria. Tiffany silver is by far the most popular nineteenth-century silver, though collectors have recently begun to turn to less expensive examples in the Art Nouveau manner, such as the ware produced by Unger Brothers of Newark, New Jersey.

Canadian silver conforms more closely to European types. Many English-speaking smiths settled in Canada after the American Revolution, and they closely followed the styles of the mother country. But there were also many French gold- and silversmiths, and they offered their own interpretations of French Rococo and Neoclassic.

Though they have used gold and silver for more than two thousand years, most Asiatic peoples have shown as much or more interest in bronze. This is especially true of the Chinese, though surviving examples indicate that Chinese craftsmen were capable, at an early period, of producing fine work in precious metals. Interestingly, the Chinese and Japanese, as well as most Indians, have always preferred silver to the more valuable gold.

The Chinese have long excelled in silver filigree work and in using precious metals as inlay in iron, copper, and brass utensils. Chinese objects made entirely of gold or silver are much more limited in form than those of the West and, like furniture, do not conform to any stylistic period.

Japanese silverwork was strongly influenced by that of China. The treasures at the Shoso-In temple, in Nara, include several large silver bowls in the Tang style. These vessels, which were probably intended as Buddhist alms bowls, are engraved with hunting scenes. They date from the eighth century and clearly reflect Japanese contact at that time with China's ruling dynasty.

However, Japanese artisans were never satisfied simply to repeat Chinese patterns. They always gave a special national quality to their precious wares, refining and simplifying foreign conceptions until they satisfied their own needs. Though larger objects were made, chiefly for temples, the Japanese preferred small things. Their silver spoons are of the best quality, and they employed gold and silver also for netsuke (tiny togglelike figures used to hold medicine pouches to men's belts) and various sword mountings.

In India gold or silver vessels could be used only by royalty or in conjunction with votive offerings. Some of the finest extant pieces are the footed betel-nut dishes from Kandy, in Ceylon (now Sri Lanka). These are finely engraved and encrusted with sapphires. Indian artisans were also adept at enameling. They traditionally used red and green enamels on gold, and blue and green on silver. Like the Chinese, the Indians favored silver filigree and inlaying precious metals in base metals.

Workers in Tibet and Siam (Thailand) employed what gold and silver was available to them in making religious articles. Statuettes and other representations of Buddha may be found, along with silver incense burners and other paraphernalia associated with religious practices.

Oriental craftsmen were familiar with most of the shaping and decorating techniques known in Europe, but due either to lack of large deposits of precious ores or to different priorities, they devoted their major efforts to other metals. Also, unfortunately, the general instability that prevailed throughout the area (except in Japan) over the past several hundred years has no doubt contributed to the scarcity of gold and silver artifacts. It is possible, though, to purchase examples of Chinese and Japanese gold and silver. Japanese sword ornaments and netsuke are widely collected and, in some cases, reasonably priced. Chinese silver cups and bowls made for export during the late nineteenth and early twentieth centuries are relatively abundant.

Of course, no objects in gold or silver can be said to be truly inexpensive compared with many other antiques. Such wares as Sheffield and electroplate silver, however, offer the opportunity to build a handsome collection with a minimum outlay of funds.

4

4
Pewter

Preceding pp.: l. to r.: Swiss pewter pie plate
with engraved and punched decoration, 17th century;
English porringer by Ingram & H., Bewdley,
18th century; Scottish pewter chalice, c. 1770.
Above: Balkan pewter flask with raised and
cast decoration, 18th–19th century. Much European
pewter followed styles prevalent in silver.

Pewter, an alloy composed primarily of tin, has long been known to metalsmiths. Its silvery sheen, so like that of the more precious metal, as well as its softness and low melting point, which permit both casting and hammer work, make pewter a desirable substitute for silver. It has in fact been referred to as the "poor man's silver."

No one knows where the metal was first worked, but, like bronze, it may have originated in the Far East. Chinese pewter mirrors dating from the Chou and Han periods (1122 B.C.–220 A.D.) have been found in graves, and India also has a long tradition of pewterwork. On the other hand, the alloy was also popular with the Romans, and Imperial pewter has been found in various parts of Europe. In England alone, more than two hundred pieces dating from 200 to 400 A.D. have been excavated.

Anyone interested in collecting pewter should recognize that, unlike bronze, which has ingredients of rather fixed proportions, pewter has been made in different ways at different times and places. Roman pewter and that of much of Europe for centuries thereafter was composed solely of tin and lead, usually 8 parts tin to 2 parts lead. The advantages of this mixture were its low cost and ease of handling, but it had drawbacks as well. The more lead, the softer and more easily damaged the article. Moreover, this metal was coarse and dull in color, darkening with age to such an extent that the pejorative term "black pewter" was often applied to alloy with a high lead content. It should also be noted that the presence of lead in this pewter created the risk of lead poisoning for those who used the utensils.

At an early date the English added other metals such as bismuth, copper, or zinc to the mixture to increase hardness and lighten color. As early as 1348, ordinances of the London Craft of Pewterers mandated that better-quality pewter (primarily tablewares) be made only of tin and brass, with no lead whatsoever. This high standard has been maintained in England ever since, and so superior was the English metal to that of the Continent during the eighteenth and nineteenth centuries that French and German pewterers frequently marked their ware "London Tin" or "English Tin," either to defraud or in honest declaration that they had obtained their alloy from England.

It was the English also who developed the form of pewter most widely used after the mid-nineteenth century. This metal, known as "hard pewter" or Britannia metal, consists of tin, antimony, and a small amount of copper. It has a silvery-white sheen, very like that of silver, and is so hard and strong that it can be readily rolled thin in presses and worked in sheets, something quite impossible with traditional pewter. Large quantities of Britannia metal were produced in England and North America during the nineteenth century, and this ware is highly collectible today. Such ware, particularly later examples, was at least partially machine made, but it was well made and can be extremely pleasing to the eye. In America, particularly, the examples most sought after are those that reflect the influence of Art Nouveau and Art Deco styling.

Despite the metal's long history, the pewter actually available to collectors is limited as to period. Roman and ancient Chinese examples are, of course, few in number and seldom appear on the market. Moreover, though it was certainly used during the Middle Ages (an edict of the Council of Winchester issued in 1076 granted churches the right to use pewter for chalices), practically no pewter exists that can be dated between the fifth and fourteenth centuries. Most pewterware available today was made in the eighteenth and nineteenth centuries.

There are several reasons for this dearth of early pewter. First, tin, the basic ingredient of the alloy, is scarce throughout most of Europe. England's preeminence in the field is due largely to the wealth of its ancient tin mines at Cornwall. Other nations had to import their tin or develop their own sources. Germany, for example, became an important pewter manufacturer only after the sixteenth century, when tin deposits were found in Saxony.

Moreover, since it was valuable, pewter was reused. When a piece became damaged or passed out of fashion, it was simply melted down and recast. Most early ware has long since gone the way of the smelter.

And finally, nearly all early pewter was cast, at least in part, and this process required as many as four different molds. These molds were made of bronze and were extremely expensive. Their cost to the craftsman, even more than guild regulations, limited access to the trade.

The guilds themselves were extremely important to the trade. Like those of the gold- and silversmiths, they regulated both access to the craft and the quality of its products. As early as 1473, England's Edward IV granted a royal charter to London's Pewterers' Company, giving it authority to control the activities of pewtermakers throughout the land. Similar guilds with comparable powers appeared at about the same time in Europe. At first many of these were joined in a common guild with other, allied trades such as smithing or marketing, but by the sixteenth century most had become independent.

The guilds' goals were always the same: to control product quality, to eliminate destructive competition (i.e., to create a monopoly), and to regulate working conditions. As with the silverworkers, one of the methods adopted to achieve these ends was the marking of ware. In 1503 the Crown decreed that all English pewter be impressed with the maker's "touch," a mark consisting of his initials or, at a later date, his full name. Similar regulations were enacted by the Continental guilds. A master sheet of marks was kept at the guildhall, so that if inferior goods

appeared on the market they could be traced to their source. This was a vital quality control, for, unlike gold- and silversmiths, the pewterers themselves, not the guild, marked the ware.

Nor were the pewterers content with a simple touchmark. Again emulating the silversmiths, they also stamped their ware with a variety of "quality" marks such as the crown, the angel, the rose, the hammer, or various combinations of these. These marks, intended to indicate the grade of the metal used, are often seen on collectible pewter. The rose and crown, for example, should reflect use of an alloy containing little or no lead. Note the phrase "should reflect," for while the marks themselves were fairly uniform throughout Europe and the British Isles, just what they stood for often differed greatly from region to region. The guilds were far less successful in controlling quality marks than makers' marks, so while English pewter impressed with the rose and crown would indeed have no lead content, French ware bearing the same mark might contain as much as 20 percent lead.

The quality marks do, however, provide fairly reliable guides to where a piece of pewter was made. The angel, for example, is always European, not English. Likewise, the rose and crown, when combined with a maker's touch containing three or more initials, reflects a Continental origin. Since this information is important, all serious pewter collectors should own one of the various directories to pewter marks. But collectors should bear in mind that owning a book and finding the marks on pieces one wishes to purchase recorded therein may not be enough. Pewter, particularly seventeenth- and eighteenth-century examples, is now valuable enough to justify faking, and more than one false mark exists.

Though usually united in a single guild, pewterers were often specialists. Plates, dishes, and similar articles were

manufactured by "sadware men" ("sad" was an early term for "heavy"), who, though they might employ molds, worked primarily by hammering to shape. The "hollowware" pewterers made teapots, bowls, and tankards, primarily by casting; and "triflers" specialized in small objects such as spoons, buckles, and buttons. Among them, these craftsmen turned out a vast quantity of pewter in many different forms. Some of these, such as baby feeders, colanders, and funnels, are quite rare today, but other types—plates, bowls, pitchers, and drinking vessels—are readily available.

Perhaps the most popular of all European pewter items are mugs and the larger, usually lidded, tankards. Clearly, tankards have existed for many centuries—there is one in a Dutch museum that is dated 1331. Dutch and German examples are particularly well known and sought after by collectors. The Dutch pieces include tankards made for members of such organizations as the shippers' and carpenters' guilds. These are engraved with the owner's name, his occupation, and his town. Another traditional Dutch vessel is the "town hall" tankard, a large drinking mug out of which honored community guests were given a greeting or farewell toast. German tankards were frequently made in forms appropriate to the owner's occupation. A shoemaker might drink from a shoe-shaped vessel, or a farmer from one that looked like a cow. Town and guild tankards were, of course, made for special purposes and in limited numbers. Consequently, they are usually difficult to find today. Most outstanding examples long ago made their way into major collections.

German pewtersmiths of the Augsburg area excelled in making *edelzinn*, or "noble pewter," which consisted primarily of tankards and giant serving flagons called *schliefkannen*. These were often more than 3 feet (91.4 cm) tall and so elaborately decorated that many authorities think

that they are actually goldsmiths' work done in pewter. But German pewterers also made less ornate and less expensive drinking vessels. During the eighteenth and nineteenth centuries they produced two standard types of tankards, tall slender ones and short thick ones. The latter are believed to have been designed for shipboard use, where their form would provide needed stability. Both types are still obtainable at moderate cost.

Smaller mugs and handleless beakers were even more common in a day when wine and beer were usually preferred to water for reasons of health as well as taste. They were made throughout Europe, and are still quite common today, as are handled measures with which the mugs are sometimes confused. The measures, however, come in graduated sizes and have a thick, banded lip that would make drinking uncomfortable.

Pewter plates are also popular with collectors, particularly the very large (16 inches [40.6 cm] or so in diameter), wide-rimmed serving dishes known as chargers. Prior to the seventeenth century most people used wooden dishes. When pewter became available to all classes during the 1600s, the first pewter dishes tended to resemble their wooden antecedents. They were usually rimless and square or eight-sided. Soon, however, a reinforcing rim was added, and the traditional circular form was adopted.

As befits their modest purpose, most pewter dishes and chargers are not decorated, though some may bear coats of arms and family initials. A notable exception are salvers, large traylike platters that had a place of honor in the homes of the well-to-do. The seventeenth-century French pewter master François Briot, considered by some to have been the greatest of all craftsmen in this medium, is known for his "temperance salvers," which were cast in elaborately carved molds and were heavily engraved with biblical and mythological scenes in the late Renais-

sance style. These pieces, needless to say, are of museum quality. But while few can hope to own a temperance salver, nearly all collectors can afford an eighteenth- or nineteenth-century pewter plate.

Other popular pewter items are lighting devices, which include candlesticks as well as whale-oil, camphene, and kerosene lamps; salt cellars; inkwells; serving dishes; and snuffboxes. The latter were very popular in the last century and are of great interest, since many were made in unusual shapes such as guns, shoes, and hats. Spoons too are very collectible. The olive-shaped bowls of the earliest pewter spoons, made in the sixteenth century, were succeeded by round and then oval bowls. Most eagerly sought after are the so-called Apostle spoons of the seventeenth to nineteenth centuries, which had handles terminating in the figure of a saint. These were given to children at Christmas—a figure of the child's baptismal name-saint formed the finial of the spoon handle. Many other, less common, pewter utensils may also be encountered.

Most collectors are interested in the way in which their pewter has been made, and this also often provides clues to the age and origin of a piece. As previously mentioned, most early pewter was cast or hammered. Cast pieces were made by pouring molten alloy into a bronze mold. Once the form had hardened it was removed and "skimmed" to smooth out rough spots on the casting. Skimming was accomplished by pressing a sharp tool against the pewter piece as it was turned on a lathe. Once the skimming was completed the pewter was marked and then buffed to a high polish using a hide-covered buffing disk and finely ground abrasive powder.

More complex pieces such as tea- and coffeepots were cast in several different sections which were then welded or fused into a single unit. Ware of this sort, which was made until around 1800, is relatively thick-walled and

sometimes shows solder marks, particularly about the base and handle.

Plates, platters, and basins were often made by hammering a cast disk of pewter into the appropriate shape. Hammering, in addition to strengthening the alloy, left tiny indentations. These marks are important from the collector's point of view, for they serve to identify the process by which the piece was manufactured. Hammer work disappeared early, and few such pieces will be found that were made after the mid-eighteenth century.

As industrialization and competition spread through the metalworking industry, pewterers looked for faster and cheaper ways to work. For many, Britannia metal, developed in the mid-1700s, provided the answer. Britannia can be rolled into hard, thin sheets that can be worked into shapes impossible to obtain with traditional pewter. At first the new alloy was cut to shape or stamped out by dies and then soldered together, a process known as seaming. Seamed Britannia is lighter and thinner than pewter and can be recognized by the soldered seams on its interior. Soon after 1800, Britannia-ware makers developed the process of spinning. This involved pressing a sheet of cast Britannia against a wooden mold mounted on a lathe. As the lathe turned, the alloy conformed to the shape of the mold. Spun Britannia is easily recognized by the concentric ridges left on its interior by the revolving form. Though some collectors of early pewter tend to look down on Britannia as a purely industrial development rather than a craft product, it is definitely collectible and can be found in many forms including coffeepots, sugar bowls, creamers, cruet stands, flagons, and pitchers. As befits its late development, Britannia is frequently marked with a company touch, such as that of Reed and Barton, rather than with the initials or name of an individual maker.

Like the silversmiths whom they so often emulated,

101

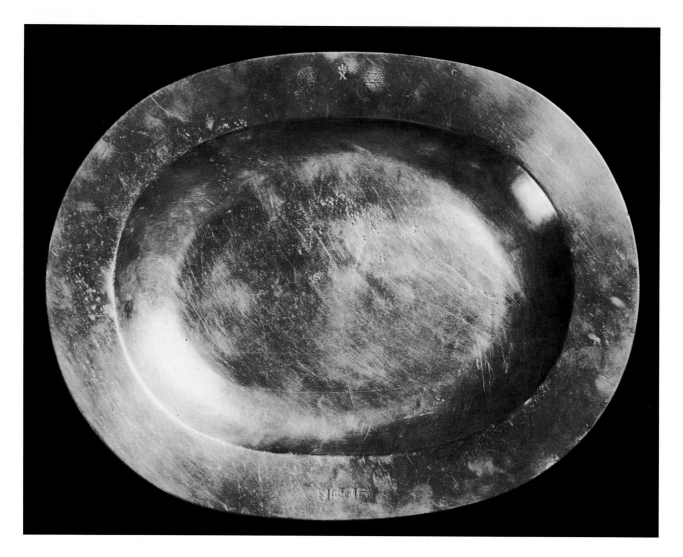

pewtersmiths were conscious of style, at least to a degree. Those who could afford it and whose customers demanded it followed the great stylistic changes of the sixteenth to nineteenth centuries. Early work betrayed its Gothic origins in bulging shapes and engraved panels. Renaissance influence was reflected in rounded forms decorated with allegorical figures; with the arrival of the Baroque the graceful Renaissance forms became heavier and ornamentation grew exaggerated. Spiral ribbed patterns and irregular, shell-shaped curves are typical of Rococo pewter, while Neoclassic shapes reflect a return to tradition with their straight lines and minimal decoration.

Much pewter, though, particularly that used by the lower classes, shows little of such change. Pewterers often made the same objects in the same way for many years. In part this was because bronze molds were simply too expensive to replace every time tastes changed. In part it

was traceable to the fact that the craft served the most conservative segment of society.

Pewtermaking reached its zenith during the seventeenth and eighteenth centuries, at the very time the pottery industry was developing in England and on the Continent. As the rich turned from pewter to porcelain and fine earthenware, the middle class replaced its wooden utensils with pewter. The burghers, merchants, and artisans were much less prone to sudden changes in taste than were the wealthy, and even when they adopted pewter vessels, they often maintained old and familiar forms. Thus, in Scandinavia, pewter tankards bore cast banding to make them resemble the wooden vessels they had replaced. Likewise, the bulging-bottomed, gourd-shaped tankards and measures were modeled on ancient leather drinking bottles. Many other pewter pieces followed the design of antecedent bronze, wood, or pottery items. It

was, in fact, not until the mid-eighteenth century that pewter truly became the poor man's silver, trying slavishly to imitate the forms of its illustrious exemplar.

In decoration, at least, pewter never equaled silver. The medium forbade it. Early pewter was much too soft for repoussé work (hammering from the inside of an object to produce a raised pattern on the surface) or its reverse, impressed decoration. Consequently, most ornamentation was cast in the mold or engraved on the surface of a piece. On certain types, such as the small, handled bowls known as porringers, cut-out designs were used.

Gilded, lacquered, and enameled pewter may also be found. Nineteenth-century Continental pewtersmiths often covered tea canisters and tobacco boxes with a thin blue lacquer and then cut designs through this to display the metal beneath. Other pieces were entirely gilded or were painted with enamels. Since it was intended to be covered, pewter decorated in this manner was often of poor quality. With the increasing interest in pewter as a collectible metal, many gilded or lacquered pieces have been stripped of their covering, only to reveal pitted or otherwise defective alloy.

Pewter decoration varies greatly from country to country. Continental European pewterers and those of the Far East used the most elaborate techniques. The English, who produced the best alloy, also employed less decoration than any other European nation. Their ware relied on simple lines, classical style, and modest engraving.

The English were pioneers in the production of pewter; but they also, more than any other group, contributed to its eventual decline. In the eighteenth century, at the very time when pewter was becoming generally available to the middle and working classes, English potters were introducing mechanized production, which soon led to the

manufacture of vast quantities of pottery and porcelain. These quickly replaced pewter among the wealthy, and it was not long before they won the favor of other groups as well. The popularity of the new materials was due in part to an effective advertising campaign. Potters pointed out the drawbacks of pewter in doggerel such as the following:

Pewter plates are not so good
Since they must be polished.
If porcelain plates are on the wood
This work can be abolished.
Set out, therefore, if you are able
Porcelain plates upon the table.

Buyers heeded this exhortation, as they did similar ones made by the expanding tin and glass industries, and by the middle of the nineteenth century, the English pewter industry had fallen upon hard times. A similar fate soon befell the Continental pewterers.

Pewter did not just vanish, however. The malleability, smooth finish, and soft gray color of the alloy recommended it to Art Nouveau stylists, so there is quite a bit of collectible English and European pewter from the late nineteenth century. William Morris, a leading figure in the Arts and Crafts movement, used the metal in everything from picture frames to hammered decorative panels.

Of the Continental pewtermakers, the Germans were perhaps the most active. The rise of the German city-states and the eventual unification of the country led to a period of great wealth and social activity. There was a need for substantial quantities of pewter, and following the discovery of tin deposits in Saxony, cities such as Augsburg, Nuremberg, and Hamburg became great pewtermaking centers. Many different items were produced, chief among them drinking vessels.

The greatest of all German pewter masters was probably Gaspar Enderlin, who worked in the seventeenth century, but the following hundred years also produced fine craftsmen such as Simon Krober of Augsburg, famous for his elaborate tiered serving pieces such as epergnes and cruet stands. Some German pewter was inlaid with copper, a technique uncommon in western Europe. During the Biedermeier period of the mid-nineteenth century, German pewterers turned out many cups and plates engraved with homely sayings. These are most collectible today.

Dutch pewter was often as elaborate as that of Germany, and the masters of the great manufacturing centers such as Amsterdam delighted in lavish decoration and outsize pieces. They were particularly well known for their massive tankards and serving dishes. Because of the close relationship between the two countries, Dutch pewterers often used English metal, and the quality of their ware frequently rivals that of their island neighbors'.

Though they too sometimes favored ''noble pewter,''

the French for the most part created more delicate and stylish wares. They employed English tin almost exclusively; and, at Paris, Lyons, and Bordeaux, they produced flagons and beakers taller and more slender than those of Germany and Holland, as well as unique helmet-shaped ewers and finely engraved salvers. As one might suspect, French pewter, particularly the better-quality pieces, followed the changing forms of silver much more closely than most other European ware. It is possible to find clearly recognizable and distinct examples of French ware from the Gothic right through the late Victorian period.

Swiss pewter was closely related to that of France. Large, spouted flagons and decorated tankards were, perhaps, the most ostentatious items; but masters like Johann Manz of Zurich also made tableware such as sugar bowls and serving dishes.

Southern European pewter, while not as abundant as that of northern Europe, was often more lavish. In Italy the major centers of production were Venice and Bologna,

and the alloy was worked in a variety of styles. Renaissance pewter was, of course, popular, but at the same time there existed a tradition of decorating ware with geometric and floral motifs clearly Middle Eastern in origin. The Italians made fine decorative plates, many of which were intended only for display, not use. These are most collectible, though the metal is sometimes soft and dark from the addition of too much lead.

Spanish and Portuguese pewter is, for the most part, ecclesiastical; relatively small quantities were made for domestic use. Spanish pewter measures, church beakers, and plates are still found in local flea markets. As in Italy, the ware often shows a Moorish influence.

English colonists brought the craft of pewtering to North America, and there was a pewterer, Richard Graves, working in Massachusetts by 1635. The trade was, however, slow to develop due to a lack of material—major domestic tin deposits were not discovered until well into the nineteenth century. The craft was also hampered by foreign trade restrictions. As early as 1601 England forbade the export of bronze pewter molds, and other regulations threatened pewterworkers with loss of citizenship if they emigrated. The laws were quite effective. One evident result of the English restrictions is that most pewter found today in the United States is English, not native, in origin.

As a general rule, collectors take the position that unmarked pewter is American. The assumption is based on the fact that, unlike their European counterparts, American pewterers were never required to mark their ware, and many did not do so. It is known, though, that despite the prevailing rules, some English and European ware was also left unmarked. Examples of these unmarked pieces have long been imported into the United States.

Much pewter made in the United States *is* marked, of course. A craftsman proud of his work was likely to mark

it even though he was not legally bound to do so. Much research has been done on American pewterers, and many of these men and the marks they used are well known to antiquarians. Unlike their English and European contemporaries, American pewtersmiths used a variety of touches, many of them purely decorative. Eagles, flags, and stars, symbolic of the new nation, were particularly popular; but one will also find anchors, as well as pelicans, griffins, and other beasts. As with all pewter, the presence of a known mark greatly enhances an item's value.

Because of the greater value of marked pieces, there has been quite a bit of mark forgery in American pewter. Unmarked pieces, both English and American, have been stamped with the ciphers of famous American pewter-

107

smiths. In some cases, completely counterfeit specimens have been fabricated, given some artificial wear, and then falsely marked. Unless one is extremely well versed in the field, it is best always to buy pewter from a reputable dealer who will guarantee the authenticity of his merchandise.

American pewter is distinguished from that of Europe by its simplicity—greater even than that of English ware. Lines were clean and simple, and even engraving is rarely found. Most early examples are of lead-based pewter, for Britannia metal was not widely available in the New World until around 1825, when the pewter industry was already becoming obsolete in Europe.

The Americans never produced "noble pewter." Their most lavish examples are a few engraved plates and church flagons. Perhaps the most characteristic American pieces are lighting devices, particularly whale-oil lamps. America was the world's greatest producer and consumer of whale-oil lighting fluid, and nowhere can so great a variety of whale-oil lighting fixtures be found.

Though it was generally replaced by tin and pottery soon after 1860, pewter continued to be made in the United States. Britannia-ware companies, particularly in New England, produced elaborately molded Victorian tea sets and tableware throughout the nineteenth century. Tiffany and Company, among others, used the metal in everything from desk sets to lamp bases. The Tiffany pieces, especially, are today regarded as choice collectors' items. Other American Victorian pewter remains undervalued and offers a good opportunity for collectors—something that might also be said for its European equivalent.

In Asia, the best-known pewter-manufacturing center was China. As previously mentioned, pewter, primarily in the form of mirrors, was made during the Han and Chou periods. Because of its heat-keeping properties, the alloy was favored then and in later times for wine pots and serving plates. It was also employed in altar sets—candlesticks and incense burners.

Much later, during the eighteenth and nineteenth centuries, Chinese pewter found a ready market in Europe. Elaborate pieces, engraved and inlaid with brass and copper or adorned with quartz, colored glass, and semiprecious gems, were made for export. This tradition continued into the twentieth century, but modern ware can be distinguished by the fact that the brass and copper, rather than being inlaid into the pewter, are soldered or appliquéd to the surface. Most common of the wares made in this manner are teapots and tea canisters.

The Japanese also employed pewter, though to a lesser extent. They used it primarily as inlay in wood and lacquerware, where it served as a substitute for silver.

India, too, has had a longstanding pewter industry. For at least the last two hundred years, Indian craftsmen of the town of Bidar have made ewers, basins, trays, and boxes that are cast, then finished on a lathe, decorated with lavish engraving, and inlaid with gold and silver in floral and geometric patterns. Bidri ware, as it has long been known, was a great favorite with the English and other Europeans who traveled in India, and examples frequently appear in Europe. It is also still available in India.

Pewter may be found in other areas of the world as well, but its greatest production has always been confined to Europe, North America, and parts of Asia. When it is found elsewhere—in South America, for example—it is a European introduction.

Though its great period of use as utilitarian domestic ware is long past, pewter continues to be made in many places throughout the world. Artisans are still drawn to its soft, silvery luster, and more and more modern craftsmen are choosing to work in the medium.

5
Bronze

Preceding pp.: Detail of Chinese bronze ceremonial
wine vessel, late Shang dynasty (13th–11th
century B.C.). The earliest bronze is from China.
Abstract decoration is typical of such pieces.
Above: Dutch bronze mortar, 1504. One of the oldest
known European pieces. Because it was durable,
bronze was often used for objects such as mortars.

Though important in the West, particularly as statuary, bronze is preeminently the metal of eastern societies. Bronze is an alloy (typically, 88 parts copper to 12 parts tin) to which other metals such as zinc or lead may be added to vary color or strength. It is relatively lightweight, dents easily, and, in the untarnished state, is of a reddish-brown hue. With age it acquires a blue-green, gray, or black patina. It melts easily, and since it is readily cast, most bronze objects are produced in this manner. While nowhere near as costly as gold or silver, bronze is not inexpensive to manufacture. Consequently, the variety of items produced in the medium over the years is considerably less than that found in iron, tin, or even pewter. There are, however, many beautiful and valuable bronze objects available to the collector.

Anyone with even the least knowledge of bronze thinks immediately of the famous archaic vessels of old China. That these are both extremely expensive and practically unattainable does not alter their great importance to an understanding of bronze manufacture.

Chinese history records the discovery of bronze as having occurred in the third millennium B.C., but the earliest known specimens date to the time of the Shang dynasty (1766–1122 B.C.). Bronze vessels of this era are found in several clearly distinguishable forms, and most appear to have been used as ritual food or wine containers. The molds in which they were cast were carved with great skill in order to produce pieces that are basically three-dimensional and linear, with an emphasis on fanciful animal forms, basketwork patterns, and geometric motifs. Shang bronzes are squat and massive, with heavy round or square bosses, or protrusions, on their surfaces.

Food vessels of this and the succeeding Chou period (1122–221 B.C.) are of two general types: those with three or four feet (tripods or tings), which were used for cooking food or warming wine; and those with a circular or ring base, used for serving. Such bronzeware was always very expensive and owned exclusively by the nobility. An ancient Chinese proverb refers to the upper class as "those who eat from bronze tripods to the music of bronze bells."

Not all Shang vessels were used for such mundane activities as eating and drinking. Most of these pieces were inscribed, and the inscriptions indicate that they were often given as royal gifts or created to mark the resolution of a dispute or the granting of a kingly privilege. And at least some pieces served more sinister purposes. Stylized ritual axes of bronze were used to behead sacrificial victims, who were entombed with deceased members of the nobility. In fact, it is only because most early bronzes were buried with their owners that they survive today.

Bronze was, of course, also used for weapons, tools, and horse and carriage fittings. This sort of bronzework is generally of less interest to collectors, particularly to the Chinese, for whom the inscriptions on early bronzes may be at least as significant as the pieces themselves.

During the Chou period the form of bronze containers gradually changed. The stylized animals, especially the grotesque monster masks that decorated many ritual pieces, took on a more naturalistic and less symbolic quality. Surfaces became smoother, shapes more gentle, and decorative devices almost minute.

Simplification in form continued during the Han dynasty (221 B.C.–220 A.D.), which some Chinese consider the last great age of bronzework. Bells that had had decorative bosses in the preceding periods now had smooth surfaces; they and other objects were often decorated with gold and silver inlay. Mirrors appeared for the first time. They were circular, never more than a foot in diameter, and their backs were decorated with geometric devices or stylized representations of hunting parties or scenes from

Chinese legends. Their reflecting surfaces were highly polished and convex so as to enlarge the image.

During the succeeding unstable period known as the Six Dynasties (220–589 A.D.), Buddhism was introduced into China from India, and this resulted in a change in the role of the bronzeworker. His product now became closely tied to the popular religion. Earlier types disappeared or were changed in form as craftsmen began to devote themselves to casting votive figures, many of which were gilded. Mirrors continued to be made, but now the decorative devices were more likely to be figures of humans or deities.

Chinese bronze sculpture, primarily of religious figures, reached its zenith during the Tang dynasty (618–906 A.D.). Both religious and secular work of this period had a profound effect on the craft as it was practiced in neighboring Japan, for the island nation had its first sustained contact with China at this time and adopted many Chinese forms and techniques.

After 1000 A.D. Chinese bronzework declined sharply in quality. Not least among the reasons for this was a general belief that the work of the Shang-Han epoch could never be surpassed. Though it may be hard to believe, the Chinese had, even at this early date, been collecting ancient bronzes for hundreds of years. Though graverobbing was punishable by death, archaic bronzes had a way of appearing in shops from time to time, and they were also discussed in great detail in eleventh- and twelfth-century literature. In fact, by the Sung period (960–1279 A.D.), the Chinese were already making reproductions of Shang and Chou bronzes! These and later reproductions usually bore the reign mark of the period on which they were modeled rather than in which they were actually made; so, as a general rule, Chinese date marks are of little help in fixing the age of their bronzes.

Chinese bronzes, though of less artistic merit, continued to be made, and religious figures as well as various types of utilitarian objects have been manufactured throughout the past centuries. Pieces made during the Ming (1368–1644) and Ching (1644–1912) periods are relatively easy to obtain at reasonable prices. Particularly popular with collectors are the archaic-type bronze vessels with gold and silver inlay that were manufactured during the reign of Emperor Chien-lung (1736–1796). Nineteenth-century types tend to be more lavishly decorated with a profusion of motifs (stylized elephants, dragons, and birds, for example) applied with little understanding of their original meaning or relationship to the form.

During the eighteenth and nineteenth centuries the Chinese made many types of bronzeware for export to the West. These included teapots and canisters, candle holders, vases, and knickknacks such as snuffboxes and sewing boxes. Nearly every sort of decoration from enameling to engraving may be found on these pieces. They vary in quality and price, but most offer an excellent opportunity to the would-be collector of Chinese bronzes.

So pervasive has been the cultural impact of China on its northern neighbor that Korean bronzework can barely be distinguished from that of China. Swords, mirrors, statues, and cooking utensils from 1300 A.D. have been found in Korean tombs, but they are so similar in style to those of China that it is difficult to determine if they are of Korean manufacture or were left by the numerous Chinese invaders. Later Korean bronzes do differ somewhat from those of China. Nineteenth-century vases are long and slender with hourglass-shaped bodies. Figures of gods and demons are characterized by the large heads and hands and short bodies found in Indian rather than Chinese work. In general, though, Korean forms are less varied and less innovative than those of China and Japan, and they are accordingly of less interest to most collectors.

1

2

Japanese bronze is quite another matter. The skills of
alloying and casting bronze came to Japan in the first or
second century B.C., probably by way of China. Certainly,
the earliest known Japanese examples, from the Asuka
period (c. 450 A.D.), are somewhat reminiscent of the
Shang-Chou examples, at least in decoration. These
pieces, known as *dotoku*, are bell-shaped objects cast in
molds and covered with hunting scenes or representations
of birds and animals native to Japan. *Dotoku* range in
height from 1 to 4 feet (30.5 cm–1.2 m); what they were
used for is not known. Possibly they were religious implements, possibly just symbols of wealth and status.
Somewhat similar objects have been found in Korean
graves of the same period.

In 538 A.D., the ruler of Korea's Pekche kingdom presented a gilt-bronze statue of Buddha to Japanese digni-
taries. This date marks both the official introduction of
Buddhism into the islands and the beginning of sustained
contact between Japan and its mainland neighbors. From
this point on, Japanese bronzes became diversified. The
earliest examples followed Korean and Chinese forms, but
native craftsmen soon modified these to suit their own
purposes. They developed two types of mirrors, one about
a foot in diameter with a handle or metal stand, and another, only 4 inches (6.2 cm) across, that had a hole in the
back to hold a hanging cord. Both types were made with
little modification right through the nineteenth century,
and later examples are still available. They also made *bon-
sho* (temple bells) in various sizes; *goko*, which are
Buddhist ceremonial objects; incense burners; musical instruments; and various household implements.

At first most Japanese bronze objects had religious significance. Most famous among these are the two Great
Buddhas at Nara and Kamakura, the world's largest figures
in bronze. By the eighteenth century, though, the Japanese

116

3

4

5

1

2

3

118

4

were making a variety of utilitarian bronze objects for both domestic use and export. The smallest of these pieces are *tsuba*, or sword guards. Elaborately cut and engraved and often inlaid with precious metals, *tsuba* have, for some years, been very popular with collectors. Larger bronzes include urns, vases, and statues. Late-nineteenth- and early-twentieth-century examples of these were deliberately made to resemble archaic Chinese designs in form and decoration, and were often "antiqued" with a coat of dark brown lacquer. Though sometimes overdecorated, these late Japanese bronzes are well made and reasonably priced.

Japanese bronzes fall into three decorative stages. Those of the first period (600–1500 A.D.) are extremely elegant, with relatively sparse but vigorous ornamentation. During the middle period (1500–1700) bronze objects were highly elaborate and rich in detail. From 1700 until the twentieth century a naturalistic school flourished, with bronze-workers emphasizing lifelike forms and exact duplication of natural features. Thus, while most objects available to the modern collector are naturalistic in form, this style does not characterize all Japanese bronzes.

Indian bronzework, particularly statuary, is of great historical importance. The north Indian Gupta dynasty, which flourished during the fourth to sixth centuries, produced magnificent votive statues. During this period priestly codes regulated the attitudes and gestures of religious images, and standard forms were created that have varied little over the centuries. Since Guptal art had great influence in Indonesia, China, and Japan, bronze casters of those lands were still making, in the nineteenth century, religious figures that looked much like those produced in India a thousand years earlier.

Indian religious images are of three types: Buddhas, the supreme beings of Buddhism, which appear clad in priest's

robes; Bodhisattvas, enlightened beings destined to become Buddhas, which are dressed as kings or nobles; and Devas, demigods and protectors of the faith, which take the form of warriors or commoners. Related to the latter are the various human and animal forms associated with the Hindu faith. All these forms have been made in bronze for generations, and smaller examples, particularly of the eighteenth and nineteenth centuries, are quite accessible to the collector.

Much early Indian bronze statuary was destroyed when the land was overrun by Islamic armies in the twelfth century. The Moors were opposed on religious grounds to images of the human form, and they destroyed all they could find. Accordingly, most available Indian statuary dates from the post-Islamic period.

But Indian bronzemakers never confined their efforts to statuary. Bazaars and antique shops in India still are filled with bronze locks (often in the shape of animals), betel-

nut cutters, and tiny cast replicas of human and animal figures. Also popular are the small, decorated bullock bells used by herders to keep track of their livestock. Larger nineteenth-century collectible bronze vessels include *lota,* or water jars, and *surahi,* elegant, long-necked, engraved ewers in which water from the sacred river Ganges was preserved. Water pipes, now so popular, were not developed until the seventeenth century, but many different forms are still being made and sold.

The bronzework of Nepal and Tibet is closely related to that of India, though it is somewhat more ornate. Nepalese craftsmen specialized in Buddhist images, many of which were gilded or inlaid with precious stones. So highly skilled were these workers that most Tibetan bronze is thought to have been made by immigrant casters from Nepal.

Indonesian bronzes, particularly Buddhist religious articles, also show the influence of Indian prototypes. Simple utilitarian objects such as bronze cooking pots and water vessels are less clearly related to mainland types, and eighteenth- or nineteenth-century specimens show Dutch influence, reflecting Holland's long domination of the island chain.

Authorities believe that bronze casting was first developed in the Middle East many centuries before the birth of Christ. Whether or not this is the case, there is no doubt that Persian and Syrian craftsmen have long produced sophisticated work in this medium. As early as the eighth century, Islamic craftsmen were making bronze trays, ewers, and drinking vessels in the shapes of animals and birds, and by the thirteenth century the Saljuk people of what is now Iran were practicing the arts of engraving and delicate inlay in silver and gold. Bowls, vases, bottles, and trays from Iran and Syria are characteristically decorated with applied or engraved arabesques, animal forms, and

120

Arabic inscriptions. Some forms, such as small boxes and inkwells, are also enameled.

Except for some recent deterioration in design, Near Eastern bronzes have changed little over the centuries, and nineteenth-century examples are of high quality. These have been imported into Europe and North America, and many can be found in antique shops.

With the spread of Islamic culture along the north African coast and into Spain, Near Eastern bronze casting techniques and designs influenced other areas. Nineteenth-century bronze door knockers in the form of a hand grasping a ball are popular tourist purchases in Morocco and Algeria. Other inexpensive nineteenth-century Islamic bronzes are animal bells, water pipes, small lamps, and knives.

Unlike north Africa, most of black Africa seems devoid of bronzework. There is, however, a single notable exception. In west Africa, within the boundaries of what is now Nigeria, there has long flourished a bronzeworking tradition of considerable artistic merit.

In 1897 a British punitive expedition, reacting to the massacre of a peace mission, captured and sacked Benin City, capital of the large Bini Empire. The invaders carried off more than a thousand pieces of sophisticated bronze. These included magnificent plaques several feet long depicting hunting, war, and processional scenes, as well as heads and animal figures.

Since Portuguese explorers had reached Benin City in 1485 and had carried on a friendly trade relationship with its powerful rulers until well into the seventeenth century, and since Portuguese soldiers appear on some of the plaques, it was initially assumed that the explorers had taught the Bini the art of bronze casting. This is no longer believed to be the case. Many of the plaques date from the sixteenth century, and it would have been impossible for

124

native craftsmen to have attained the level of sophistication evidenced in their execution within such a short time. Moreover, the pieces are typically African, reflecting an interest in capturing not the visible appearance of an object but rather a stylized interpretation of what the artist believes to be its spirit.

It is now thought that Islamic traders brought the bronze craft to Nigeria, though possibly not directly to the Bini. Bini legends describe it as having been learned from Iguegha, a bronzesmith sent to them by the king of Ife, a city located about a hundred miles north of Benin City. Support for this story was first obtained in 1910, when a life-size bronze head was excavated at Ife. In 1938 several more such heads were discovered within the city, and now nearly thirty are accounted for. The Ife heads are extremely sophisticated castings done in a naturalistic manner generally quite different from anything else known in Africa, including all but the earliest Benin work. They date to the thirteenth and fourteenth centuries and are thought to be the forerunners of the later, more stylized Nigerian bronzework.

Most Nigerian bronze is now in museums or private collections, but any collector interested in bronze should be aware of it, for it ranks among the finest work in this medium ever done anywhere.

Bronze crafting has long been practiced in Europe. The Greeks and Romans were skilled at it, and their heritage came to full flower during the Renaissance, when Italian masters created both statuary and luxurious household items. Best known are the herculean images by such sculptors as Donatello and Verrocchio. Their subject matter was the human figure, typically represented as a god or hero. The work was extremely naturalistic, and the metal was chemically treated to produce a patina like that found on excavated ancient bronze. The originals of most

125

Renaissance bronze figures are of only academic interest to collectors, for they are seldom available at any price. However, bronze casters have for centuries been producing respectable replicas of the more famous Renaissance pieces, and these often can be purchased quite reasonably.

European bronze falls into two categories—those items made for practical purposes, and those made for appearance only. Utilitarian items are on the whole earlier in development. Since bronze is stronger and resists fire better than copper or brass, it has long been used for cooking equipment. The Romans used bronze cauldrons and three-legged, long-handled cooking pots. Both types persisted into the nineteenth century, particularly in rural areas of central Europe. Weights and measures of all kinds have been produced in bronze; in England these are often associated with specific towns where they constituted the official standard.

Bronze mortars have always been popular, for the metal is sturdy enough to withstand constant pounding. For the same reason, doorstops and knockers were often made of bronze. European and English examples of these objects are among the most popular collectibles.

Luxury items in bronze are quite another thing. In Italy, Renaissance craftsmen made elaborate candelabra, candlesticks, and caskets inlaid with gold and silver. During the eighteenth and nineteenth centuries, clock cases, perfume sprinklers, bells, jugs, and hand mirrors were produced. Like objects of gold and silver, bronzes of high quality followed the prevailing stylistic trends. Thus we can find bronze in every mode from Renaissance to Victorian.

Certain European bronzework stands out. During the fifteenth and sixteenth centuries the German craftsmen of Saxony made elaborate aquamaniles, large ewers used to pour water over guests' hands at the conclusion of each

course during a banquet. Some aquamaniles are in the form of a mounted knight, others take the shape of fabulous animals such as dragons or unicorns.

Some of the finest of all bronzework were the gilded bronze (ormolu) furniture fittings produced in France during the seventeenth and eighteenth centuries. The French also manufactured elaborate bronze andirons and fireplace tools. Among the most collectible western European bronzes of a later period are the various small objects produced in the Art Nouveau style during the last years of the nineteenth century. These pieces were cast in commercial foundries and made in sufficient quantity to still be obtainable. They range from ashtrays and nut dishes surmounted by nymphs with flowing hair to slim candlesticks in the shape of flowers.

Though sculptors in every age and in every part of the world have occasionally turned their attention to animals, it was not until the nineteenth century that there developed a school of artists who made them their major interest. A group of French sculptors, aptly called *Les Animaliers,* attempted to break the classical grip on their field by turning to what they perceived as more naturalistic animal forms. The foremost of these artists was Antoine Louis Barye (1795–1875), who promoted the scientific study and exact duplication of animals. He was followed by others like Georges Gardet and François Pompon. Pompon, who specialized in birds, took a somewhat impressionistic approach to his subject matter.

The *Animaliers* differed from their predecessors in more than subject matter. They came at a time when bronze foundries were becoming industrialized and were developing techniques by which they could produce duplicates of any statue in various sizes and in any desired quantity. Thus, for the first time in history, bronze statuary became available to the public at a price most could afford. Nineteenth-century factory pieces of this sort are of fine quality, and they are readily obtainable in the antiques market. Other things being equal, the most desirable examples are those bearing the names of the sculptor and the foundry where the piece was produced.

Of course, bronze was used in Europe for many things besides statuary. In Venice, at the same time as Renaissance sculptors were creating their greatest work, bronzemakers were manufacturing bowls, jugs, and trays modeled on Syrian and Persian examples obtained in trade.

The Islamic influence was even more marked in Spain, where the Hispano-Moorish style in bronzework remained prevalent long after the expulsion of the Moors at the end of the fifteenth century. Even today, Spanish bronze weapons, bowls, pitchers, and caskets are inlaid and engraved in the tiny geometric and floral patterns favored by Moorish craftsmen. The Rastro, Madrid's famed flea market, is still a source for Islamic-influenced bronzes, many of them made in the nineteenth century by gypsy artisans.

Naturally, the Europeans brought their styles and techniques in bronze casting to their colonies in the New World. To what extent the craft was practiced, however, often depended on the local availability of material. The Portuguese and Spanish possessions in South America were rich in both copper and tin, and the pre-Columbian peoples had worked these metals to a limited extent. Delicate bronze implements have been found in Peruvian graves, and a small cast-bronze plaque of unknown purpose was found in Argentina. Once the Europeans arrived they manufactured bronze as they needed it, primarily for altar furnishings and candlesticks to be used in the many churches they built. Europeans were much more interested in gold and silver, though, and the amount of South American bronze is not extensive.

Nor is there much early North American bronze, though for very different reasons. Until the middle of the nineteenth century, when substantial tin deposits were discovered in the United States, tin had to be imported at high prices. Consequently, American founders worked primarily in copper and brass. Some bronze skillets from the late eighteenth and early nineteenth centuries are known, but the most common American bronze items are bells and spoon molds. With the discovery of tin and the development of factories in the 1860s, however, all this changed. Bronze foundries in the United States soon rivaled those of Europe in their technical sophistication. Well-to-do Americans seemed to need everything from duplicates of Renaissance statues to ormolu mounts for their furniture to gigantic bronze candelabra in the best Louis XVI manner. The factories supplied their needs—often too well, for some American bronze (which was not always marked) so closely resembles European prototypes as to be nearly indistinguishable.

Not all American bronze was copy work, though. American craftsmen excelled at Art Nouveau design, and their bronzework in this mode was outstanding. Between 1902 and 1918, Tiffany Studios produced a vast array of bronze objects ranging from desk sets and candlesticks to lamps (including electrified ones), jewelry, and vases. Many of these pieces were inset with glass or silver, and all were carefully made. Other manufacturers created similar objects, and today "Tiffany type" bronze objects are among the most popular of all American collectibles. Moreover, while signed examples and lamps are expensive, other pieces can sometimes be obtained at moderate prices.

By virtue of its age, history, and beauty bronze remains today, as it was thousands of years ago, one of the most important of metals. It is fortunate that so many desirable objects in this metal can still be found.

6

6
Glass

Preceding pp.: American pressed Sandwich glass
vases, *c.* 1850. These vases were made at
the well-known Boston and Sandwich Glass Company
in Massachusetts. Above: Russian
glass locket, 19th century. Locket contains two
miniature portraits, a man
on one side and a woman on the other.

The making of glass is so complex that it is difficult even to envision how the process might have been developed or, more likely, discovered. Yet it is one of the oldest crafts, although its early practice was limited primarily to Europe, the Near East, and Asia.

Glass is a hard but fragile substance composed of silica (obtained from common sand) and an alkali, usually potash or lime. When these ingredients are heated together, they melt and fuse to produce a viscous near-liquid that can be stretched and shaped while it is still hot.

It is quite possible that glass was discovered by accident—perhaps when someone mixed sand and potash in the course of cooking or building a fire. In any case, it was not long before uses were found for it. By the end of the eighteenth Egyptian dynasty (c. 1559–1319 B.C.) glass vessels were being made in some numbers. These pieces were produced by wrapping strips of molten glass around a damp sand core shaped in the form of the object to be made. When the glass cooled, the sand was washed and scraped away. The technique was slow, and the resultant ware was so expensive that relatively little must have been produced. Today only a few specimens from tombs exist as evidence of these early efforts.

By the first century A.D. a more efficient method of manufacture had been developed. The Romans poured hot glass into molds made of stone or metal. When the glass cooled, the resultant vessels were more or less uniform in size and shape. The use of molds greatly reduced the time and effort required to make a piece of glass and no doubt increased the amount made, for Roman archeological sites often contain large quantities of broken glass objects.

After the collapse of the western Roman Empire in the fifth century, glass continued to be made in Constantinople, capital of the eastern Empire, as well as in surrounding states such as Syria. The craft, however, largely disappeared in Europe except for tiny shops located in what is now the Black Forest area of Germany. There, coarse, dark green glass vessels were made for centuries. But it was nearly a thousand years before European craftsmen again attained the quality of Roman glass.

The manufacture of glass is a subtle process, dependent on the proper mixture of silica and alkali, and requiring special ovens. The first of these ovens (such as one dating to 1400 B.C. that was excavated some years ago in upper Egypt) were large, cavelike, rectangular brick structures in which open fires were built. The ingredients of the glass were placed in large clay pots and heated in the oven until molten. The process was slow and inefficient, and the glass did not always fuse properly, since there was no way of maintaining a constant temperature.

It was not until the 1800s that better ovens were devised. These had two chambers, a lower one that served as a firebox and an upper one in which the pots of melting glass (known as batches) were placed. By the eighteenth century this oven, too, had been improved on with the development of a three-tiered oven containing a firebox, a melting chamber, and, on top, an annealing oven in which finished objects were placed so that they could cool slowly without breaking.

The actual making of glass objects is an art. As mentioned, the Egyptians built up their pieces over a sand core, and the Romans employed molds. Around 300 B.C., the Syrians invented the blowpipe, which led to the development of blown glass. The blowpipe is a long, hollow iron rod. The glassblower inserted it in a pot of molten glass and removed a glob of the material, known as a gather. By blowing through the pipe he could expand the gather, much as a child blows a soap bubble. Since glass is extremely pliable when hot, the expanded gather could be shaped into anything from a plate to a bottle.

The invention of the blowpipe led to the creation of many different types of glass, each with its own unique shape—since each piece was individually formed, no two were ever quite alike. However, blown glass could not be made as quickly as the molded product and lacked the latter's uniformity. In an attempt to obtain the advantages of both methods, glassmakers combined the blowpipe with molding. The glassblower inserted the gather at the end of his pipe into a small, cuplike vessel called a dip mold. As it expanded, the blown glass took on the shape of the mold. The interiors of these molds were often carved with patterns, and these designs would be impressed on the expanding glass—hence the name pattern glass. By the nineteenth century there were many different kinds of molds, including hinged molds that could be opened for easy removal of the finished vessel.

In the 1820s, American glassmakers invented mechanical glass presses. Hot glass could be fed into these and then stamped into various shapes. At first, only relatively flat objects like plates and saucers were made, but later the presses were used to manufacture a wide variety of hollowware, such as bowls, decanters, and serving dishes. The development of pressed glass marked the real tran-

sition of glassmaking from a handicraft to an industrialized process, for while some glass is still handmade, most ware today is produced by automatic blowing and pressing machines.

Glass is decorated in several ways. Facets and grooves may be cut into it by pressing the piece against an iron wheel attached to a turning lathe. Once the glass is cut to the desired pattern it is smoothed with powdered pumice and buffed to a high polish. The brilliance of cut glass can be akin to that of a diamond, and pressed-glass manufacturers have always attempted to duplicate this quality in their products. However, since the pattern in a mold can never be as sharp as edges cut with a wheel, pressed glass can always be distinguished from cut glass by running one's finger over a piece. Both cut and pressed glass are quite popular with modern collectors. The former is, of course, more valuable since it is not only more attractive but less common as well.

Akin to cutting is engraving. Tiny copper wheels or a needlelike diamond-pointed stylus are used to cut shallow designs into the surface of a piece of glass. In some cases figures or scenes may be created, in others a background of minute dots (known as stippling) is achieved by tapping the diamond stylus with a tiny hammer. Somewhat similar results may be accomplished by etching. In this process the piece is covered with wax, then a design is scratched through the wax with a sharp steel point. Hydrofluoric acid is then applied to the glass, and it eats slightly into the exposed surface, creating a shallow pattern. Etching is faster and cheaper than engraving.

Many of the decorative techniques used with glass appear to have originated in the Near East. In the ninth century, Syrian glassblowers discovered that by adding manganese to a batch they could remove the impurities that produced common aqua or green glass and achieve a clear, colorless glass. They cut and engraved this to resemble rock crystal, a hard mineral that for centuries had been shaped into everything from cups to sculptured figures.

In the thirteenth century, again in Syria, craftsmen developed enameled and gilded glass. Enamel is itself a form of glass consisting of silica, minium, and potash mixed with various metallic-oxide coloring agents. This mixture is melted and applied to the surface of the glass. When it hardens, it fuses with the glass. Gilding is achieved by applying liquid gold instead of enamel. The Syrian glassmakers carefully painted blown-glass objects with gold or enamel to produce spectacular pieces of art. The most famous centers of this work were Damascus and Aleppo, and the most famous examples of it were Egyptian mosque lamps—large oil lamps that hung by chains from the ceilings of mosques. These lighting fixtures were enameled in various colors and frequently bore gilded inscriptions from the Koran. Though widely used in Egypt from the 1300s on, most mosque lamps were made in Syria.

The finest Syrian enameled glass was made prior to the invasion and destruction of Damascus in 1400, but the technique continued to be used, and collectors may obtain attractive examples dating to the eighteenth and nineteenth centuries. These later pieces are characterized by subordination of individual motifs to an overall decorative effect, with design elements arranged in intricate patterns based on the repetition of a single motif.

As a result of its contact with the Near East through trade, the Italian city-state of Venice became an important glassmaking center in the eleventh century. By the thirteenth century Venetian glass was being sold throughout Europe. Venice's reputation for producing some of the finest glassware in the world has continued to the present.

The earliest Venetian glass factories were located in the city proper, but following several fires the industry was relocated to the neighboring island of Murano, where it remains today. At first the glassblowers of Venice relied heavily on techniques learned from Syrian craftsmen, but in time they developed their own distinct styles. As in Syria, clear glass in imitation of rock crystal was an early product (c. 1400). However, since Venetian glass was more malleable than the early Near Eastern glass, it was also shaped into fanciful forms such as fruits, flowers, and figures. Such pieces, made during the Renaissance, are among the finest early European glassware.

Enameling was also imported from the East, and the enameled and gilded glass of Venice has a warm, soft quality particularly appealing to collectors. Other techniques such as cutting and engraving were also employed, but Venice is best known for three types of glass: millefiori, latticinio, and aventurine.

Millefiori (which means "a thousand flowers" in Italian) is the name given to a type of decorative glass first made by the Romans and rediscovered and brought to perfection by Venetian craftsmen. It is made by fusing together long, thin rods of multicolored glass to form what is called a cane, then cutting across this to reveal a patterned cross section. The cut sections are placed side by side and fused together, then they are reheated and blown to the desired shape. Cups, bowls, and other small articles were made in this manner. Venètian millefiori generally employs light-colored canes against a purple or deep violet background. Millefiori items are still made in Venice, particularly jewelry and small objects such as paperweights.

The Venetians employed opaque white glass (known to us as milk glass) both for making complete vessels and as a decorative device. While their milk-glass objects are not considered very significant, their decorative glass, known as latticinio, is of great interest to collectors. Latticinio is created by weaving thin threads of white glass into and around a clear glass matrix to produce a "candy-cane" appearance. The white threads may be plaited or filigreed, and by twisting the hot glass one can create a spiral effect. Ewers, vases, and candlesticks made in this manner are particularly attractive.

Aventurine glass was first manufactured in Venice around 1600. Copper or brass filings were scattered through a mass of transparent hot yellow or brown glass so that vessels made from the batch sparkled as though showered with gold. The term "aventurine" refers to the resemblance of this glass to aventurine quartz, a mineral. Though this ware is seldom made today, nineteenth-century examples are readily available.

Venice's only real rival for supremacy in Italian glassmaking was the town of Altare, near Genoa, where French glassmakers settled in the fourteenth century. During the following three centuries Altare produced a substantial quantity of fine glass. Since the techniques employed at these two centers were essentially the same, and since the wares were usually not marked, it is frequently impossible to tell Venetian from Altare glass.

Though Venetian glass is better known, German glassmakers can boast of a more ancient heritage. As previously mentioned, it was in Germany that the secret of glass manufacture was preserved after the fall of the Roman Empire. For hundreds of years tiny shops turned out *waldglas*, or forest glass, which was traded as far south as Spain. This ware was characteristically green in hue due to an abundance of iron-based impurities, and decoration, where present, consisted only of applied blobs and ribbons of glass. Though most early examples have long since vanished, fifteenth- through eighteenth-century *waldglas* exists in some quantity and has recently begun to attract the attention of collectors. A most interesting form of this ware is the *roemer*, a large Rhenish wineglass with a cylindrical bowl atop a long, hollow stem.

During the sixteenth century craftsmen and products from the Italian glasshouses made their way into northern Europe, and German glassblowers began to imitate Renaissance glass of the sort made in Venice. By 1650 German manufacturers had begun to employ enameling, though their interpretations of design and decoration were distinctly different from those of the South. The most popular Germanic themes were armorial—the coats of arms and heraldic devices of the various ruling houses of central Europe. One of the best-known types is the *alderglas*, a tall, cylindrical drinking vessel with or without a cover. *Alderglases*, which date from the sixteenth to the eighteenth centuries, characteristically bear an enameled representation of the double eagle standard of the Holy Roman Empire. On the outstretched wings of the eagles, fifty-six armorial bearings appear, one for each member of the Empire. Other popular pieces of the period are *humpen*, large enameled beakers that were shared by several drinkers, and elector glasses, beakers decorated with representations of the current emperor of the Holy Roman Empire and the seven electors who had designated him.

Until about 1850 most German enameled glass was ex-

Left: Chinese opaque white-and-red glass snuff bottle, 19th century. Snuff bottles served a practical purpose, but in China they were also miniature works of art on which great care and skill were lavished. Right: Indian mold-blown bottle, Rajesthan-Kota style, late 18th century. Similar in form to European case bottles, this piece was probably made in imitation of a European example. Scenes on all four sides depict European couple against a Continental landscape.

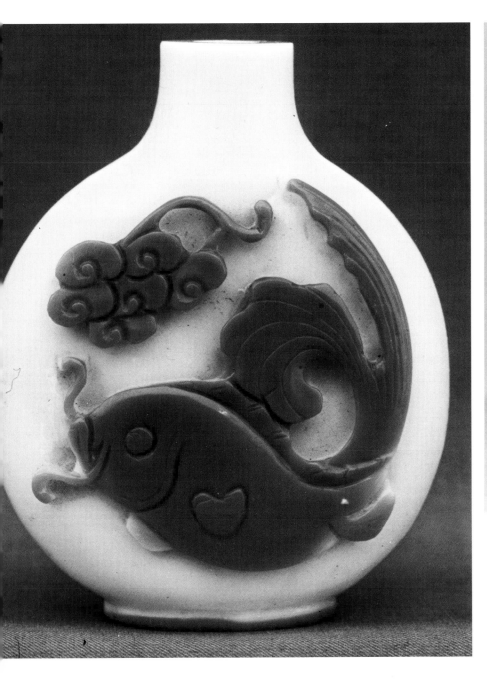

pensive and limited to the few forms described above. In the mid-nineteenth century, though, glassworkers began turning out large quantities of enameled vases, bowls, pitchers, and drinking vessels in Renaissance and Baroque styles for sale to the general public. This ware was made until the First World War, and its bright and cheerful decoration, featuring flowers and peasant figures, has made it most popular with collectors.

The Germans made more than enamelware. In 1676 they developed a fine crystal glass with a potash-lime base that came to be called Bohemia glass, owing to its wide use in that area. This glass proved particularly suitable to engraving and cut decoration, and by the end of the seventeenth century German artisans were doing wheel engraving of a quality unrivaled since the days of the Near Eastern glass masters.

The major centers for engraving were Cassel and Potsdam. In 1695 Franz Gondelach of Hesse was appointed chief glassmaker to the Landgrave, Carl of Hesse-Cassel, and until 1716 he worked at the Landgrave's factory in Cassel. Gondelach is generally regarded as the foremost of all German engravers, and his works are highly prized by museums and private collectors. He did monograms, trophies of arms, portraits, and elaborately carved goblets, most of them in the Baroque style prevalent at the time.

At Potsdam, the first glass shop was established in 1679 under the patronage of the Elector of Brandenburg, Friedrich Wilhelm. The director was Johann Kunckel, who, incidentally, is credited with the discovery of ruby glass, a lovely red ware achieved by the addition of gold chloride to the glass batch. The factory at Potsdam lasted until 1890, but it is best known for its eighteenth-century cut and engraved work, much of which was done and signed by H. F. Halter. Among Halter's more popular pieces are goblets and tankards with domed covers. These are usu-

ally decorated with engraved and gilded military motifs, including coats of arms, portraits, armorial devices, and allegorical sayings. Halter and others at Potsdam also made ware decorated with engraved landscapes, and these are among the finest examples of all German glass.

Germanic craftsmen had one great rival in the area of engraving—the glassworkers of the Netherlands. Though little is known of Dutch and Belgian glass prior to the sixteenth century, it is evident that by the early 1600s Venetian glassworkers were active in several areas of the Low Countries. Clear and colored glass with enameled decoration may be traced to this period.

By 1650, though, Germanic forms and techniques had become dominant in the Netherlands and Belgium, and engraving was widely practiced. At first this was diamond-point work, but by 1690 engraving with the wheel in the German manner had become popular. This, in turn, was replaced in the eighteenth century by a new method of stippling with a diamond point. Such skilled engravers as Anna Roemer Visscher developed an original, calligraphic style that was used to depict fruit, flowers, and insect life. In the eighteenth century, the engravers David Wolff and Franz Greenwood created diamond-stippled, engraved portraits and still lifes based on contemporary prints. Among the pieces so decorated were beakers, pitchers, and a Dutch version of the *roemer*.

Swiss glass closely resembles that of Germany, for the nation's first known glassworks, founded in the seventeenth century, was staffed by immigrants from the Black Forest. Swiss glass of the period from 1600 to 1800 is chiefly of two kinds, enameled and engraved. In each case decoration and form clearly reflect Germanic influence. The usual drinking and serving vessels are found, as well as interesting engraved or etched windowpanes bearing family coats of arms.

The rise of the English glass industry is largely traceable to the efforts of one man, George Ravenscroft (1618–1681). In 1673 Ravenscroft was hired by the Glass Sellers Company of London to build several glass factories and to undertake research in glassmaking. The fruit of his labors was flint glass (so named for the burnt flint that was used in the early formula), which he patented in 1676. Flint contains potash and lead oxide, and the addition of the lead makes flint glass the clearest and most brilliant of all glass. Though too soft for fine engraving, flint glass was perfectly suited to cutting. By the end of the seventeenth century there were more than a hundred English manufactories producing cut flint glass, and by the middle of the nineteenth century English cut glass dominated the world market.

Chief among the English flint-glass centers was Bristol, where cut-crystal tableware and decorative pieces such as vases, decanters, and candlesticks were produced. Bristol is also known for its milk glass, which was made to imitate porcelain—it is characteristically very smooth and as translucent as fine china. It is found in the form of vases, mugs, scent bottles, and salt cellars, and is often decorated with enameled birds, flowers, and figures in the Oriental manner. Most collectible pieces date to the late eighteenth and early nineteenth centuries. Other glasswares made here include marbled slag-glass mugs and flasks, which incorporated glass of several different hues; blue glass, which is often gilded; and a threaded glass similar to Venetian latticinio.

Though inferior to that of Bristol in quality and workmanship, the glass of Nailsea has a special place in the hearts of some collectors. From 1788 to 1873, the Nailsea glassworks produced a wide variety of decorative glass intended to appeal to country people. Items included miniature coach horns, round colored glass balls known as

witch balls (these were believed to ward off witches if hung at doors and windows), novelty canes in latticinio, and two types of rolling pins. The more common of these were simply solid implements made of black or green glass flecked with white, but the Nailsea works also produced hollow, colored glass rolling pins that were intended to be given as gifts. Their interiors were filled with tea or sugar, and their surfaces were enameled with quaint inscriptions such as "Welcome Home" and "The Token of Jack's Safe Return to His True Love." The striking and rather primitive quality of Nailsea glass has made it popular with some English and American collectors.

Another nation known for its cut glass is France, where the Compagnie Cristalleries factory was founded in 1818 at Baccarat. Baccarat glass is still made, and the company has long been known for its fine cut-crystal table services and its faceted prisms and pendants for chandeliers. Though expensive, Baccarat is eagerly collected. Another well-known French cut-glass center was Clichy, a suburb of Paris where a crystal factory flourished from 1840 to 1870.

The best known of all French glasswares is the paperweight. Paperweights were first made at St. Louis in the Vosges Mountains sometime around 1820, and the earliest dated example is one from St. Louis marked "S.L. 1845." During the late nineteenth and early twentieth centuries, weights were made at various other shops as well, including Baccarat (generally regarded as having produced the finest examples) and Clichy.

Paperweights vary in size and shape; most are no more than 2 or 3 inches (5–7.6 cm) in diameter. Various techniques are employed in their manufacture. Some are made of overlay or cased glass, produced by covering a clear glass core with a layer of colored glass and cutting through this to produce a contrast. Other examples are made of

clear glass formed around porcelain cameos in the shape of animals, flowers, or human heads. These cameos, which appear silver through the glass, are known as sulphides. Still other weights feature sections of cut-glass cane in the Italian millefiori style. Cutting and faceting are often added as further embellishments. The finest paperweights are so intricately and skillfully designed that they are considered miniature works of art, and few will deny French preeminence in this field.

French glassworkers were also known for their lamp work, a technique still in use. Employing various tools and a small lamp to soften the glass, craftsmen carefully shaped miniature figures and objects, some no more than a few inches high. Nevers, where glassmaking has flourished since the sixteenth century, has long been a center for such work. Another is Toulouse, where glassblowers made novelty items such as horns, drums, canes, and miniature hats. Miniatures are readily available and are of great interest to many collectors.

Glass was also made in many other areas of Europe. Russia, Poland, and other eastern European countries produced a great deal of enameled glass featuring floral and animal motifs and primarily intended for use in peasant homes. Spain and Portugal specialized in blown glass. The most characteristic Spanish example is the *porrón*, a drinking vessel with a long spout. Wine is drunk from the *porrón* by tilting the vessel so that a stream of liquid flows into the drinker's mouth without his lips touching the spout. *Porróns* have long been popular with collectors and tourists visiting Spain, though most examples sold in the flea markets and antique shops are not very old.

Europe was also an important center for the making of art glass. In the late nineteenth century, technical advances in the glass industry, such as the development of chemical coloring agents and more refined ovens, enabled glassmakers to produce a wide range of glassware in unusual forms and colors. Unlike most previous glass, this ware was intended more to be looked at than to be used, and therefore came to be called art glass. Also unlike most other glass, this ware was made in limited editions and was usually signed or marked by its manufacturers. Art glass is collected with great zeal on both sides of the Atlantic, and prices in this field are soaring.

Foremost among European art-glass makers are Gallé, Daum, and Lalique, all from France. Emile Gallé, regarded as the greatest French glassmaker of the late nineteenth century, founded a business that was active from 1897 to 1935. Though at first he experimented only with new colors, Gallé's primary interest was in glass decoration. He developed a technique for dripping enamel or multicolored glass into his pieces, and he created a variety of rich, sinuously shaped ware in the Art Nouveau style. Gallé's work is usually signed in gilt or brown enamel.

The Daum brothers, August and Antonin, established their factory at Nancy in the 1890s. They were to some extent imitators of Gallé, but their opaline glass and acid-etched floral and scenic decorative motifs were of the highest quality. Their ware is often marked "Daum-Nancy."

The Lalique factory, established in 1905 by René Lalique, is still active. This factory also started out producing ornamental glass (lamps, vases, and bowls) in the Art Nouveau style, but in 1911 the company was given a contract to make perfume bottles for Coty, and this sharply changed its focus. Lalique still makes perfume bottles today, and these stylish vessels are among the most valuable of utilitarian collectibles.

Austria also had major art-glass manufactories. In the 1880s Max Ritter von Spann, grandson of the founder of the Lotz factory in Klostermühle, obtained the formula for iridescent glass from a former employee of Tiffany and Company, which had created this type of glass. Thereafter, the Lotz shop produced Tiffany-like vases, tablewares, and decorative items. Many of these are marked "Lotz-Austria," but unmarked specimens may be confused with Tiffany glass. Indeed, because Tiffany glass brings much higher prices, there have been instances of the Tiffany signature being forged on Lotz pieces. Before it closed during the First World War, the Lotz factory also made some fine examples of aventurine glass.

In England, the best-known producer of art glass was Webb and Sons of Stourbridge. This firm developed a high-quality cameo glass in 1874 and also manufactured Burmese glass—an opaque ware containing gold and uranium oxides and ranging in hue from pale yellow to rich pink. The color and satinlike surface of Burmese made it particularly suitable for decorative ware like vases, candlesticks, and desk sets.

The American glass industry lacked the centuries-long tradition of its European counterpart, and the early days of the craft were difficult indeed. Though there was a glass factory at Jamestown, Virginia, as early as 1608, it was more than a century before the first successful firm was established. This was due in part to difficulty in obtaining raw materials and skilled workers (many countries forbade glassblowers to go abroad) and to the expense of operating a factory. In larger part, however, it reflected the restrictive policies of the English colonial government, which was more interested in selling glass to the colonists than in assisting them to make their own.

The first major American glassworks was established at Philadelphia in 1739 by a German immigrant named Caspar Wistar. Wistar's works, which lasted until 1780, made primarily utilitarian wares: window glass, lampshades, and many different kinds of bottles—including wine,

mustard, and blacking containers—from a half-pint to a gallon in capacity. Wistar's advertisement in the *Pennsylvania Chronicle and Universal Advertiser* for July 31, 1769, listed these and other wares and appealed to the patriotism of prospective buyers by pointing out that "as the above mentioned glass is of American manufacture it is clear of the duties Americans justly complain of, and at present it seems particularly in the interest of America to encourage her own manufactures. . . ."

The common glass made by Wistar is the sort most early American glass factories produced. There was little need—or time—for the manufacture of fancy glass in the new land, and what little eighteenth-century American glass is available is primarily utilitarian. An exception, however, must be made for the factory of John Frederick Amelung, which was built near Fredericktown, Maryland, in 1787. Though Amelung made common glasswares, he also produced some extremely fine engraved crystal of a quality comparable to that being made in Germany and Holland. Quite a few examples of this ware have survived, including pokals, or covered goblets; glasses; and beakers. These frequently bear identifying inscriptions such as the following, taken from a covered glass: "Made at the Glass Manufactory of New Bremen in Maryland the 23rd January, 1789 by John Fr. Amelung & Company." But Amelung's engraved glass was not a typical American product. The eventual failure of Amelung's business may well indicate that he was ahead of his time, for it was some years before American manufacturers could devote much energy to any glass other than the most utilitarian.

The industry did prosper, though, and by the 1820s glasshouses existed from New England to the Midwest. They made many things: crystal goblets of native flint glass; pressed-glass plates, bowls, and pitchers of green or aqua glass decorated with the "lily-pad" pattern now so

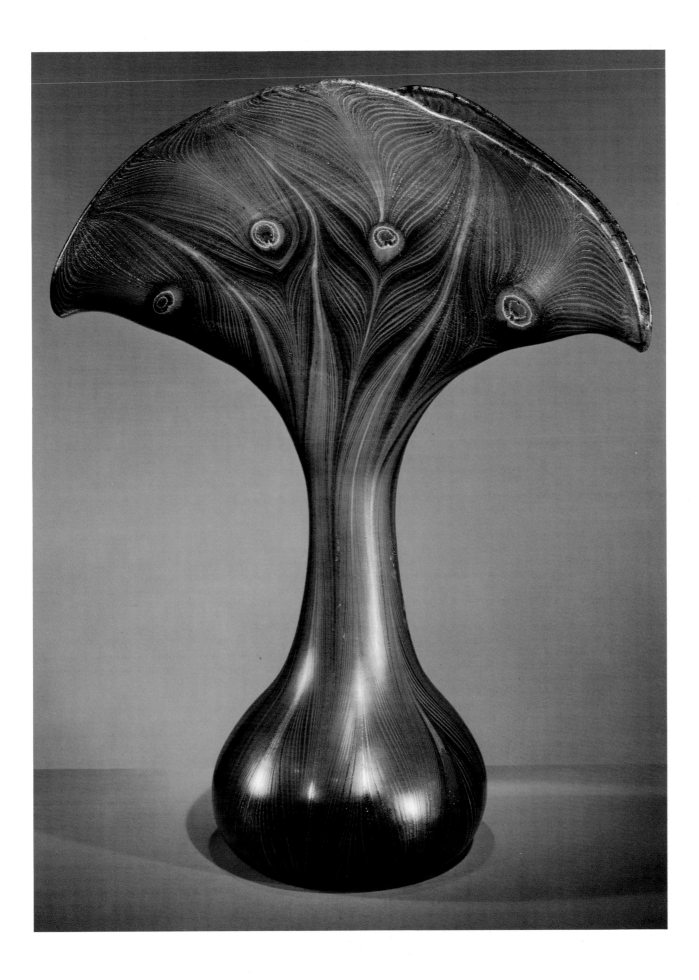

eagerly sought after by collectors; and, of course, bottles.

Americans were among the first exponents of advertising, and much promotion was done through bottles. Soon after 1800 mold-blown medicine bottles appeared, with the names of products and their makers blown into their surface. Between 1810 and 1910, when strict new food and drug laws put an end to the industry, merchants produced tens of thousands of different remedies. Called patent medicines, these concoctions relied for their efficacy primarily on alcohol or narcotics. For example, Richardson's Vegetable Bitters was recommended for "dyspepsia, sensation of weight, eructions and wandering pains." It might not have cured these maladies, but if you drank enough of it you probably wouldn't care—it was 59 percent alcohol. Likewise, Mrs. Winslow's Soothing Syrup was an efficient quieter of restless children. It should have been. One of its main ingredients was opium.

Shortly after the Second World War Americans began to collect these old medicine bottles, and today bottle collecting is a major American hobby. Since many bottles can be purchased for next to nothing or even found in old dumps, this is an ideal hobby for the young or the impecunious.

Not all American bottle glass is quite so inexpensive, however. Historical flasks, for example, were made from 1810 to 1870 as whiskey flasks, and most bore molded likenesses of political figures or patriotic symbols. These bottles, which came in many different colors and interesting shapes, have been collected since the late nineteenth century and can be quite expensive. A rare example was recently sold at auction for a sum sufficient to purchase a fine house and lot.

As the nineteenth century progressed, American glassmakers began to produce much more than bottles. They were early innovators in the pressed-glass field, and pressed tablewares from such well-known factories as the Sandwich Glass Works at Sandwich, Massachusetts (1825–1888), are regarded as highly collectible. Perhaps the most popular of these pieces are the tiny, lacy cup plates with impressed scenes or portraits of historical figures. These were used for drinking tea in the days when the tea was poured into a saucer to cool and then drunk from the same receptacle.

Americans were also among the most inventive in the field of art glass. In the 1880s Americans created several new types of colored glass, such as Amberina, patented by Joseph Locke of the New England Glass Company, and Agata, a whitish-pink glass developed by Joseph Webb of the Phoenix Glass Company. A mere listing of the various new hues developed in the United States would serve little purpose, for the effect American glassmakers had on the industry worldwide went far beyond that. First and foremost, they were innovators. They developed not only new colors, but new methods and new forms. By 1900, American glass was being exported throughout the world.

The contributions of others notwithstanding, one man is generally regarded as being the foremost American glassmaker of the late nineteenth and early twentieth centuries. He is Louis Comfort Tiffany (1848–1933). Trained as a painter, Tiffany had a strong sense of color and design, and he was attracted to the Art Nouveau style early in his career. In 1885 he founded the Tiffany Glass Company, and in 1893 he established his own glassworks in New York City. Employing the most talented craftsmen and the best materials, Tiffany became famous for his naturalistic forms and leaded glass as well as for his iridescent glass with its characteristic metallic luster. Between 1896 and 1920, the Tiffany firm produced glass so fine that many pieces went directly to museums, while others went to Europe to be copied eagerly by Continental glassmakers. Today Tiffany wares, particularly marked examples, sell for sums comparable to what one might pay for a fine painting.

Though developed at an early period, glass for many years played a subordinate role in Asia. Even in China, where it was being made as early as the period of the Three Kingdoms (221–261 A.D.), it was for many centuries regarded only as a cheap substitute for gemstones. Opaque green or white glass was cut and shaped to look like jade or other precious stones. It was only with the coming of the westerners that the Chinese recognized that there was a market for glass vessels.

In 1680 a major glass factory was established at Peking (hence the name "Peking glass," which was applied to much Chinese export ware of the eighteenth and nineteenth centuries). For many years the chief artisan at Peking was one Master Wu, a man famous for developing milk-glass bowls and vases that looked so much like porcelain that they could be distinguished only by experts.

The Chinese are also well known for their snuff bottles, the best examples of which were made during the Chien-lung period (1736–1796). Some snuff bottles are carved to imitate gemstones, others are of colored glass that gives the appearance of jade or opal. Still others have enameled or painted interiors. The snuff bottle is a highly prized artifact both in China and in the western world—so much so, in fact, that copies are common. Particularly troublesome are twentieth-century reproductions of the examples with painted interiors. These are, however, usually so poorly painted that they can fool only a novice. Other interesting Peking glass, no more than a century old and readily available in the West, includes paperweights, cigarette cases, pinboxes, and many different kinds of beads.

Glass was made elsewhere in the Orient as well. The Japanese made, in this century, fine glass beads to imitate pearls, and the Philippines have long been famous for their delicate lamp work.

Though difficult to produce, glass, because of its beauty and utility, remains one of mankind's most important achievements.

7

7
Pottery
and
Porcelain

Preceding pp.: French porcelain jardiniere and
vases with underglaze decoration, produced
at Sèvres Manufactory, late 18th century. Sèvres
is considered by many to be Europe's best
china factory. Above: Danish stoneware jar by Ove
Larsen for Bing and Grøndahl, Copenhagen,
early 20th century. An example of fine art pottery.

Except for wood and stone, no material is more readily available to the craftsman than common clay. As a result, pottery objects are among the most widely found and commonly collected of all antiques. This, however, is not the case with porcelain, which, though related to pottery, has some significant differences. It is important to have a clear understanding of the distinction between the two.

There are many different kinds of pottery, but all are made from clay. One type of clay may be used alone, or several kinds may be mixed together. Clay is found naturally throughout most of the world, and long ago it was discovered that it could be dug, refined, and baked to produce a hard, more or less waterproof substance suitable for everything from cooking utensils to statuary.

There are two basic types of clay, earthenware and stoneware. Earthenware, by far the more common, fires or bakes to a brick-hard, relatively porous body varying in color from red to pale yellow. It takes well to casting and is easily decorated, but it is quite fragile. Stoneware is baked in special kilns or ovens at a high temperature to achieve a rock-hard, watertight body. It is extremely durable but somewhat more difficult to decorate than earthenware.

Porcelain (or china, as it is often called in allusion to its origin), unlike pottery, is not the product of clay alone. It is composed of various mineral ingredients. There are two distinct types of porcelain, and each is made from different components, mixed according to complex chemical formulas. The first of these is "true" porcelain, or hard-paste. Originally made in China in the seventh century B.C., it is composed of kaolin, or China clay, combined with petuntse, an aluminum silicate. Hard-paste porcelain is baked at a very high temperature to achieve a white, more or less translucent, glassy material. Though long known in China, the formula for hard-paste was not developed in Europe until the early eighteenth century.

Early European porcelain was of the soft-paste variety, which is made from finely ground glass and clay. It is baked at about 2,012° F (1,100° C), as opposed to the 2,372° F (1,300° C) required for hard-paste and stoneware. Soft-paste porcelain is also white and translucent, but it is much more fragile than hard-paste. This characteristic, combined with various technical problems in production, led potters to abandon its manufacture in the early 1800s.

Pottery is decorated in many different ways. In societies that never developed kilns and where the pottery was burned at a very low temperature in an open fire or even just sun-baked, decoration might consist of designs scratched on the surface or painted on after firing. Decorative designs might also be applied to the surface of the pottery in the form of separately molded bits of clay, or a pot might be pierced and stamped. Mixtures of ashes or oil could also be rubbed into the surface to seal it and give it a shiny appearance.

Pottery baked in a kiln was usually glazed, both to make it impervious to water and to provide decoration. Glazes are mixtures of various substances, such as lead or ground glass, that are painted on the surface of a piece of pottery prior to firing. In the course of baking, these substances melt and form a glassy coating over the pot. Lead-based glaze, perhaps the most common of all, produces a clear, vitreous finish through which the natural color of the clay may be seen. It is also possible to add various coloring agents to the lead in order to achieve a colored glaze. In Europe, the most commonly employed ingredient was tin ash, which produced an opaque white glaze ideally suited to serve as a background for decoration.

Earthenware glazed in this manner has gone by different names at different times. In Renaissance Italy, tin-enameled earthenware was painted blue, green, yellow, orange,

and purple, and was called majolica, in the belief that it had been developed on the Spanish island of Majorca, though the technique is of Near Eastern origin. Beginning in the seventeenth century, more refined clays and a wider spectrum of colors were used throughout Europe in ware called faïence or, in England and Holland, Delftware. The only real difference between majolica and faïence is that the latter was fired twice, once at high heat to bake the clay body, the second time at a lower temperature to fuse the applied colors. Since many pigments are destroyed by the high temperatures necessary to bake clay adequately, the use of a second, milder, firing enabled faïence manufacturers to achieve a greater range of hues than had been possible with majolica.

Stoneware presents different problems. It must be fired at such a high temperature that it can be glazed only with salt, which, if thrown into the kiln at the proper moment, will vaporize and cover all exposed surfaces with a glassy finish. Moreover, of all coloring agents, only cobalt (which produces blue) and manganese (which produces black or brown) can stand the extreme heat. As a result, stoneware, which is gray or tan in its natural state, is characteristically decorated in blue or brown.

Hard-paste porcelain is glazed with a compound of lime and petuntse, which results in a colorless, glasslike finish. Soft-paste is coated with a lead-base glaze. Both are often decorated with designs in various colors that are applied either before the initial firing (underglaze) or after that and before the second firing at a lower temperature (overglaze). Because of all the skill and expense required to manufacture it, porcelain has been made in a relatively small area of the world and is far less available to collectors than is pottery.

Though the ceramic arts can scarcely be said to have originated in the Orient (indeed, the great age and wide-

spread incidence of potting makes it impossible to pinpoint its origin), they certainly flowered there, and no place more than in China.

Chinese red-and-black pottery dating to 3000 B.C. has been found in tombs, and by the Shang-Chou period (1766–221 B.C.) Chinese potters were making fine white earthenware vessels that closely resembled bronze objects of the same epoch. Examples of such ware are, of course, primarily of academic interest, for few collectors can ever hope to own them.

By the time of the Tang dynasty (618–906 A.D.) Chinese pottery was being influenced by Near Eastern metalware, for there was substantial trade with that area, and Greek motifs as well as a three-colored glaze (green, yellow, and brown) appear. Forms became more varied and sculptural as figures such as horses, men, and even stoves were made. These figures have, however, caused collectors much heartache. Because of their beauty and rarity, many reproductions were created during the eighteenth and nineteenth centuries. More than one collector has paid a small fortune for what he thought was a Tang horse, only to find that it was not even two hundred years old. As with all areas of antiques, the best protection against making such mistakes is to buy only from reputable dealers who will stand behind their wares.

The Sung dynasty (960–1279 A.D.) is generally regarded as the classical period of Chinese ceramics. Many different types of earthenware were manufactured, including fine stonewares such as Kuan, or Imperial ware, a grayish pottery tinged with blue or green, and Tzu-Chou, which was covered with white or dark brown slip (a mixture of clay, water, and pigment) incised, carved, or painted in contrasting colors. Tzu-Chou was everyday ware intended for use by the common people, and surviving examples often bear humorous inscriptions like "Don't talk among crowds," and "Go home early if you have nothing to do."

It was also during the Sung period that the making of celadon ware rached its peak. Celadon is a predominantly blue, green, or gray earthenware with an extremely thick, almost lardlike, glaze. It is so closely associated with the Chinese ceramic tradition that when most collectors speak of Chinese pottery it is to celadon that they refer. Celadon was made at least as early as the Tang era, but it was during the Sung period that it was first exported in large quantitites. Only recently, several hundred pieces have been found in the Philippines, and there is no doubt that other early celadon can be found in the Orient. Collectors should, however, note that later reproductions of the ware are quite common.

The modern era of Chinese ceramics (1400–1900) has produced wares quite different from those of the earlier periods. Whereas earlier ceramics were decorated primarily with incised or impressed designs over a thick glaze, giving a carved, jadelike effect, Ming (1368–1644) and Ching (1644–1912) pottery is noted primarily for painted decoration, both underglaze and overglaze.

It was also during these later eras that Chinese export of pottery to the West reached its peak, and European and American collectors are presented with a veritable treasure trove of seventeenth- to nineteenth-century Chinese ceramics. The chief form of this export pottery was Fatshan or Shekwan ware, which had a hard red or gray stoneware body glazed in streaky red, blue, green, or white. It was used primarily for vases, flowerpots, and figures of people, birds, and animals.

Though important in its own right, this export pottery took a back seat to Chinese export porcelain. As previously mentioned, the first Chinese porcelain appeared in the late Tang period. By the Sung epoch, two types of thin, translucent porcelain, Ting and Ying Ching, were being

made, primarily at Ching-Te-Chen, a town in southern China that has been one of the world's leading porcelain-manufacturing centers for centuries. These early porcelains were plain white or off-white, hues that were refined during the Ching epoch with the development of *blanc de Chine,* an ivory-white china without the greenish or bluish tinge common to ordinary white porcelain.

Early Chinese porcelains were largely undecorated, but with the expansion of the western market the Chinese created under- and overglaze chinas that have long been famous among Occidental collectors. Chief among these are *famille verte,* which is predominantly green; *famille noire,* with a black ground; *famille jaune,* on a yellow ground; and *famille rose* (the most popular), in which floral patterns in white, green, and other shades are painted on a rose-pink background. Many collectors see a distinction between *famille rose* Canton (a type of ware made throughout southern China), which has primarily floral decoration, and rose medallion, which is ornamented with figures and motifs within a central frame. Both forms are popular and available in the West, as are the Canton and Nanking porcelains decorated with blue willow patterns.

Korea, too, has a long ceramic history, though it has been seriously disrupted from time to time by war and internal upheavals. During the twelfth and thirteenth centuries the Koreans produced the famous Koryo celadon with decoration incised or inlaid in contrasting clay and an unusual crackled glaze seldom seen in Chinese celadon. Korean potters also made stoneware and porcelain, both decorated in an underglaze blue. Other than some examples from the Yi dynasty (1400–1900), few of these wares remain.

There is much more Japanese pottery and porcelain. Though the Japanese did not begin to make porcelain until the sixteenth century, they have produced a vast quantity in the last four hundred years. Among the best-known types is Imari, a brightly colored china with multihued floral centers surrounded by a brocaded border pattern. Imari became so popular with westerners that the Chinese copied it for export during the nineteenth century. Imari was made at the town of Arita, a famous pottery center that is also known for Nabeshima and Kakiemon ware, both of which are extremely fine and very expensive porcelains. Another highly regarded Japanese china is Kutani, which is primarily green in color and often decorated in brown, red, and yellow. Kutani is still made today. Many collectors consider Japanese porcelain made between 1900 and 1950 to be an excellent investment, for though it is now plentiful and inexpensive it will not always be so, and its high quality will certainly draw continued attention. Kutani and the well-known Noritake porcelain are believed to be among the better purchases today.

The Japanese have always preferred pottery to porcelain, and they have made many interesting types, most of which are characterized by a rustic charm and poetic appeal that has led western studio potters to copy them extensively. Such tiny towns as Hirado and Arita, as well as larger communities like Kyoto, have produced many different examples of stoneware and earthenware. Many of the earlier pieces are associated with the tea ceremony; tea kettles, cups, and storage vessels are prominent among these. Though not generally collected in the West, Japanese earthenware is highly prized by discriminating native collectors.

Much Chinese and Japanese pottery and porcelain is marked, usually on the base. Late marks, such as "China" or "Made in Occupied Japan" give a reliable indication of age, but the various reign marks and potters' marks found on many pieces, both early and late, often have no relation whatever to the age of the ceramics, and no one should

attempt to date pieces on this basis alone.

The Pacific islands, notably New Guinea and Australia, produced fire-baked pottery, some of which was decorated with incised designs of faces or painted with native pigments. This ware was made through the nineteenth century. Used primarily for cooking and eating, it was always made by women and decorated by men. Probably the best examples come from the Fiji Islands, where bowls, jars, and oil lamps were given a glazelike coating of resin.

Islamic potters employed a great variety of glaze and decoration techniques. The earliest known pottery from the Near East is Gabri ware, which was made in Persia and dates to the tenth to thirteenth centuries. It is a red earthenware covered with a white slip through which dec-

orative designs are cut to create a two-tone effect, a technique known in the West as as sgraffito. A later form, Samarra ware, made in the fourteenth century, is essentially a faïence, indicating that Italian and Spanish potters may well have learned this technique from Moorish artisans.

Syrian and Persian potters were well known in the seventeenth and eighteenth centuries for their *kashi*, or enameled tiles, which were used in the construction and decoration of homes and mosques. These tiles were decorated by cutting designs (which might be anything from Arabic characters to large floral compositions) into the clay and then glazing it with yellow, brown, purple, blue, or white slip.

Though early multicolored tin-glazed ware is also known, the Turkish pottery with which westerners are most familiar is the blue-and-white underglaze ware— plates, mugs, and jugs—manufactured during the eighteenth and nineteenth centuries. The designs are finely executed, generally in an asymmetrical arrangement. Stylized flowers, such as tulips and roses, appear, as do geometrical patterns and human and animal figures. Much of the decoration indicates the influence of Chinese ceramics.

The variety and quantity of European pottery and porcelain are so great as to make it practically impossible for any collector to have more than a mere sampling, even of the wares of his own country. Of all the types in existence, the pottery most readily available today is the so-called peasant ware—earthenware and stoneware made quickly and inexpensively for sale to the common housholder.

In Germany and England this is often stoneware. Potters in such towns as Raeren and Grenhausen in the Rhineland area of Germany began making stoneware in the sixteenth century and continue to do so today. Among the

158

commonly seen examples are large tan or gray stoneware jugs with relief and incised decoration highlighted by blue-slip glaze. Of greater interest to collectors, however, are the salt-glazed steins, mugs, and tankards made here and in other areas of Germany. The impressed or applied decoration on these drinking vessels, often featuring knights or biblical figures, is of such high quality that it has been favorably compared with the finest German Renaissance art. Stein collectors are so numerous in Europe and the United States that they have formed their own organizations.

Another form of collectible stoneware is the Bellarmine jug, a Rhenish vessel with a bearded mask molded into the front. The term "Bellarmine" comes from a fancied resemblance of the mask to the face of Cardinal Bellarmine, a sixteenth-century Catholic cleric hated in Protestant countries. Similar pieces, known as "graybeard" jugs, were made in Fulham, England, during the 1700s.

The English also made utilitarian stoneware with a light tan glaze and decoration applied by running a toothed wheel around the piece before firing. This brown stoneware was most abundant during the mid-nineteenth century, and it is now quite popular as a decorative item in England and the United States.

England produced finer stoneware as well. From the late eighteenth to the middle of the nineteenth century, potters at the well-known center of Staffordshire manufactured attractive small figures of children and working-class people to be used as mantel ornaments. Some of these were made of earthenware covered with lead glazes, but many others were of salt-glazed stoneware. Prominent among these figures are the so-called Toby jugs, small pitchers made in the shape of a squat, fat man wearing a three-cornered hat. All Staffordshire figurines are of great interest to present-day collectors.

Early European earthenware production was centered in the South, particulary in Italy and Spain. The most famous Italian center for the manufacture of majolica was Faenza (whence comes the name faïence), where the ware was made as early as the fifteenth century. The first tin-glaze ware made here and at other potting towns such as Orvieto was decorated in green and purple; at a later period blue and yellow were preferred. Faenza ware is characterized by its strong color, excellent form and proportion, and the high quality of the decorative drawing on its surface. Potters still work at Faenza, and over the years they have turned out many tiles, plates, vases, jars, and platters. The latter are often decorated with religious or mythological paintings set off in panels known as reserves.

Spanish majolica and the later, more colorful faïence were, of course, strongly influenced by Moorish form and decoration. During the eighteenth and early nineteenth centuries the greatest Spanish faïence center was at Alcora, near Valencia. Alcora tin-glazed earthenware was characterized by highly sophisticated pictorial painting. There is still an active folk-pottery tradition in Spain, and much fine glazed earthenware is made at places such as Alcora, Toledo, and Seville.

The French also made faïence at various centers, including Rouen, Strasbourg, and Sinceny (in the northwestern department of Aisne). Ware made at Sinceny—figures, vases, bowls, and plates—had a whiter glaze than is ordinarily seen on French faïence. Sinceny pottery, which is often marked with an S or SCY, is very popular with collectors.

The coming of the machine age and even the twentieth century did not put an end to the European pottery tradition. Stoneware is still made, both practical utilitarian vessels and designer-executed wares such as those of Denmark's Bing and Grøndahl factory. Bing and Grøndahl pot-

Opposite: Italian majolica plate, blue with
gold luster, Deruta, 16th century.
Majolica was introduced into Italy from the
Near East and brought to perfection
in the Faenza area. Below left: Russian
statuette of a balalaika player,
early 19th century. Russian porcelain,
especially that of St. Petersburg, is of high
quality. Below right: German hard-paste monkey
by Johann Kaendler of Meissen factory,
18th century. Germans were first in Europe to
learn how to make hard-paste porcelain; Meissen
factory was first of its kind in Europe.

tery is already highly collectible, though much of it is only a few years old.

As previously mentioned, porcelain came late to Europe. Many specimens had been obtained from China, but for a long time Europeans were unable to produce their own porcelain because they did not know how it was made. Chemical analysis proved too difficult, and the Chinese refused to divulge their formulas and ingredients. However, the westerners were not without resources. Alchemists had, by experimentation, discovered the secret of soft-paste porcelain in the seventeenth century, and in 1708 Johann Böttger, a German alchemist and ceramic technician, arrived independently at the correct formula for hard-paste. He developed a suitable porcelain glaze in 1709, and the following year the Elector of Saxony established the renowned Meissen porcelain manufactory and appointed Böttger to manage it. From 1710 until today, Meissen has produced fine-quality porcelain. Its products are known in England as Dresden china, in France as Saxe.

Meissen is characterized by elaborate painted enamel decoration. Miniature landscapes, harbor scenes, birds, and Oriental foliage cover pieces that follow the prevailing styles in silver. Meissen figures were also well known. Johann Kaendler, a celebrated modeler, worked there from about 1731 to 1775 and almost singlehandedly created what is now regarded as the European style of figure modeling. Early Meissen is, of course, quite expensive, but nineteenth- and twentieth-century examples are obtainable for reasonable sums, and like their predecessors, they are of high quality.

In the 1730s a strong rival to Meissen presented itself in the form of Sèvres, a French porcelain factory established at Vincennes and later moved to the town of Sèvres. The first porcelain made here was of the soft-paste variety, but after 1769 hard-paste was manufactured. Sèvres decoration was characterized by diminutive painted figures and flowers set in panels against richly colored backgrounds. The pottery at Sèvres still produces high-quality china.

And, of course, there were and are many other noted European porcelain centers. Italy's Capo di Monte porcelain manufactory flourished at several different locations during the late eighteenth and the nineteenth centuries. Its beautifully modeled figures of folk types, clerics, and commedia dell'arte characters are very much in demand among collectors.

In Russia, the Royal Imperial Porcelain manufactory began making hard-paste porcelain in 1762, and the works have been active almost continuously since then. Best known of the pieces from this shop, located at St. Petersburg (now Leningrad), are modeled figures of Russian peasants and dishes painted in the Neoclassic style.

Even Ireland produced high-quality china. Best known is Irish Belleek, a glazed, marblelike porcelain with a pearly luster. Though Belleek was not developed until the 1860s, it has become one of the most collectible forms of porcelain.

Since porcelain has always been expensive and limited in quantity, nearly any nineteenth-century example is collectible and many later pieces are already being traded at well above their original cost.

As might be expected, the pottery of North America, particularly those pieces made during the years of settlement, closely resembles that of Europe. In what is now the United States, potters were active as early as the 1630s, but nothing of this early work survives. Documents indicate, however, that these early artisans worked primarily in earthenware, suitable clays being generally available throughout New England and along the Atlantic

coast. The forms made were those needed by an expanding and relatively primitive society: cups, bowls, plates, crocks, and jugs. A few less common pieces such as toys, whistles, and inkwells were also produced. Decoration, for the most part, was rather ordinary. Much of the ware was simply lead-glazed, allowing the natural body color to show through. Potters with more time, skill, or ambition glazed their ware in combinations of various hues such as red, green, brown, and yellow. The combination of black splotches on a red body was particularly favored in New England.

What appeared rarely in American earthenware was the opaque white of tin-ash-glazed earthenware. America simply has no tradition of faïence, even though many of the potters certainly had some knowledge of the technique and large quantities of European Delft were imported during the eighteenth and nineteenth centuries.

The most elaborately decorated American earthenware was the slip and sgraffito ware produced primarily in the Germanic areas of Pennsylvania, Virginia, and North Carolina. Potters in these regions who were familiar with middle-European peasant pottery designed elaborate pie plates, sugar bowls, and other pieces on which names, dates, and pictures were incised and painted in multicolored slip. Designs were also cut through the slip to create a contrast between the coating and the red or yellow clay beneath it. Such pottery, called sgraffito ware, is uncommon today and in great demand among collectors of Americana.

Stoneware was also produced in early America. There were stoneware clay deposits scattered along the Atlantic coast, and by 1750 there were kilns from New York to the Carolinas. Most of the ware was produced by craftsmen of English or German descent, and the products tended to resemble European examples. American pieces were,

however, never so lavishly decorated. Ornamental designs, which were incised into the wet clay and then painted with blue slip, were employed until the 1830s, but only in rare cases did they reach the level of sophistication seen in German steins and presentation pieces.

After 1830, most American stoneware potters decorated their work with elaborate designs, either floral or of a topical nature—flags, slogans, or pictures of political figures, for example. This decoration was painted on with a brush and was usually in cobalt blue, though manganese brown is occasionally seen. The characteristic working style was a free-flowing abstract line that owed much to Spencerian Script, an elegant style of business writing and drawing taught in many American schools in the nineteenth century. Though based on European antecedents, this decoration is truly native in development and is today regarded as an important form of American folk art.

The best known of the other traditional American wares is Rockingham, a ceramic consisting of a yellow clay base glazed in various shades of mottled brown. Though it originated in England in the eighteenth century, Rockingham was brought to its fullest development in the United States. Particularly well known are the products of the mid-nineteenth-century pottery at Bennington, Vermont. Bennington ware may be found in every form from candlesticks and cuspidors to finely modeled animals. Especially well regarded are the lions, deer, and cows that were modeled on English examples.

There is a relatively small amount of early American porcelain. The first attempts at production, such as those of Andrew Duché in the eighteenth century and the firm of Tucker and Helme in the early nineteenth, ended in failure, and it was not until the mid-1800s that American manufacturers overcame the twin devils of lack of captial and foreign competition. Between 1850 and 1900 several

major factories were established, including Ott and Brewer of Trenton, New Jersey, the Union Porcelain Works of New York, and Knowles, Taylor and Knowles of Liverpool, Ohio. Ware from these shops generally follows European forms and decoration and is, of course, most collectible.

Another important area of American ceramics is the work of the art potter. As the nineteenth century drew to a close, the first large pottery factories arose, eclipsing individual craftsmen. Around the turn of the century, a few individuals with backgrounds in the fine arts began producing highly sophisticated pottery and porcelain objects that were handcrafted, often one of a kind, and intended to be valued more for their beauty than their utility. This ware, which came to be known as art pottery,

varies greatly in quality and design; but work by the more highly thought-of potteries, such as J. B. Owens, Weller, and Rookwood, commands a high price despite its lack of great age.

Canada's pottery shows the dual nature of that country's population. Stoneware was made almost exclusively by potters of English origin, or, after 1850, by American potters who had migrated north. Consequently, most Canadian stoneware closely resembles that of the United States in form and decoration. There is little blue-decorated ware prior to 1860, and later pieces are often indistinguishable from American ware unless they bear the name of a Canadian manufacturer. Canadian earthenware is a different matter. In the English-speaking provinces it was made in the English manner. In areas with a predominantly French population peasant ware of the sort still seen in rural France was common. These pieces tend to be rather heavy, with minimal decoration. A notable exception, however, is the limited amount of Canadian slip and sgraffito earthenware that was made by colonies of German immigrants.

Nearly all of the pre-Columbian societies of Central and South America produced pottery. The great majority of this ware was sun-baked or fired at very low heat. What such specimens may have lacked in durability, they more than made up for in decorative variety. Pre-Columbian potters produced everthing from ritual figures to an array of household utensils. Most of these pieces were elaborately decorated. Some, such as the bowls made by the people of ancient Peru, were ornately paneled, either before or after firing. Other specimens were decorated with incised designs or applied elements. Still others were made of pieces of clay that were cut to shape and fitted together prior to baking. Much of this pottery is of very high quality, and it is of great interest to modern collectors and historians.

After the arrival of the Europeans, Spanish and Portugese techniques were imposed on the local traditions. Native potters, using European kilns, created quite respectable examples of majolica and other traditional Continental ware. At the same time, many of them continued to make pottery in their own way and for their own use. Even today, most Central and South American countries can boast of native potters producing high-quality traditional ware.

The continuation during the twentieth century of a strong art- and folk-pottery tradition in nearly every nation, be it advanced technologically or not, makes it clear that potting is indeed one of the most important of all crafts.

8

8
Metalware

Preceding pp.: American weathervane by
Cushing and White, Waltham, Massachusetts, *c.* 1860.
This weathervane was modeled after a trotter
named Ethan Allen. Above: Chinese miniature copper
bottle decorated with a design inlaid in
gold, 18th century. The Chinese often embellished
copper utensils with gold or silver inlay.

Copper, brass, iron, and tin have been the metals of the common people for generations. Frequently referred to as base metals, to distinguish them from the precious ores, they have at times been employed by the wealthy for a variety of purposes from weapons to decoration. However, these materials have served primarily utilitarian ends—as kitchenware, builders' hardware, and storage containers. For the most part, ware in these mediums was made in great quantity, for the need was great; and great quantities survive, making copper, brass, iron, and tin objects among the most available and least expensive of all antiques.

Copper, the lightest of all workable metals other than tin, is also, after iron, the hardest. Its malleability is its chief asset: it can be both cast and beaten. Though there is no documented proof, there is little doubt that copper was the first metal to be discovered and used by man. It was being employed in China and the Near East long before the Christian era, and its role as the major component of both bronze and brass has long been recognized.

It is obtained by both surface and deep mining, and while not the most difficult substance to separate from its ore, the mining and refining of copper can scarcely be called a pleasurable occupation. As recently as the 1700s the work was backbreaking drudgery, as eloquently described by one chronicler of life in the English copper mines: "The first stage [in the cleaning of copper ore] is to throw aside the 'deads' or rubbish with which the ores are invariably intermixed. This process is cleverly performed by girls of seven or eight years of age, for three pence or four pence a day. The largest fragments of ore are then 'cobbed' or broken into smaller pieces by women. Then, after being again picked up, they are given to the maidens, as the Cornish people term girls from sixteen to seventeen years of age. The maidens 'buck' the ore with a bucking iron or flat hammer, by which they bruise the rock to sizes not exceeding the top of a finger. The ores are now given to boys who 'jig' them or shake them in sieves under water by which means the ore or heavy part keeps to the bottom while the 'spar' or refuse is scraped from the top."

And this was but *one* of many stages in final production of the metal. It took more than 12 tons of ore (and how many children, no one knows) to produce a single ton of refined copper.

Highly rust-resistant and an efficient heat conductor, copper has long been favored for cooking and heating utensils. However, the metal is not without its drawbacks. Copper imparts an unpleasant taste to food cooked or served in it, and some believe it to be poisonous as well. This concern was of sufficient moment for the Swedish senate, in 1753, to prohibit the use of copper vessels by the army and navy.

To some extent the criticism of copper may have been a competitive device, as may be surmised from a pamphlet issued in 1755 by an English tin manufacturer, appropriately titled *Serious Reflections Attending the Use of Copper Vessels:* "The great frequency of palsies, apoplexies, madness and all the frightful train of nervous disorders which suddenly attack us without our being able to account for the cause or gradually weaken our vital faculties, are the pernicious effects of this poisonous matter taken into the body insensibly with our vittles and thereby intermixed with our blood and juices." Wherever the truth may lie, it has long been customary to coat the interior of copper cooking pots with tin.

Brass, like bronze, is an alloy of copper, usually 2 parts copper to 1 part zinc. The more zinc, the lighter the golden hue of the brass. Brass is heavier and has a harder, more wear-resistant surface than copper. It takes a high polish, is easily joined, and is admirably suited to casting.

Though long known to metalsmiths, it did not assume a major industrial role in the West until well into the eighteenth century. This was because early brass had to be made by combining granules of copper and calcined calamine (impure zinc) in a cauldron. It was necessary to heat these substances to the point at which the zinc would melt and combine with the copper in a lump, which could then be shaped into a small ingot. The process was slow and yielded little alloy. In 1781, an Englishman named James Emerson developed a process for directly fusing copper and zinc in large quantities, and this led to a rapid increase in the availability and use of the ores.

The manufacture of brass objects was also encouraged by the development, in the mid-nineteenth century, of the process of spinning, a technique also used with silver and Britannia metal. Thin cast-brass disks were pressed against wooden forms revolving on a lathe until they conformed to the shape of these molds. Most brass kettles and basins found today bear the telltale interior concentric circles associated with spinning.

No metal has been more crucial in the growth of civilization than iron. Found in abundance in many different parts of the world and extracted with relative ease from its ore, iron, both cast and wrought, has a long history. It was first used at least three thousand years ago, and the Chinese are known to have levied a tax on it as early as 700 B.C.

Since both cast and wrought iron have been made for so many years, collectors are likely to encounter both forms frequently, and they should be familiar with the characteristics of each. Cast iron is iron in a relatively impure state, containing as much as 4 percent carbon, which makes it hard but brittle. Consequently, it can be cast in molds but not shaped by blacksmiths' tools. Wrought iron, on the other hand, has been refined by heat

and pressure to remove nearly all its carbon, leaving a malleable substance that is readily worked at the forge and is characterized by great toughness and elasticity.

Wrought iron is often the more interesting to collectors because of its wider distribution and the greater artistry that has gone into its creation. A blacksmith was limited in ironworking only by his supply of raw material and his skill. Taking a bar of crude iron and heating and hammering it until its consistency suited him, he would use hammer and tongs to shape it into anything from a spearhead to a cooking pot or doorlatch. Each piece of wrought iron is hand done and thus unique.

Cast iron was produced in foundries, which were limited in number, and by casting, which assured that all pieces of a particular type would be more or less similar in form and appearance. The first step in casting an object was to carve a wooden pattern in the exact shape of the item to be produced. This pattern was then either pressed into wet sand on the foundry floor or placed in a rectangular, sand-filled wooden box called a flask. In either case, once the pattern was removed an impression was left, and into this was poured molten iron, which then cooled and hardened in the desired shape. Though this method was effective, making the wooden patterns was costly and time-consuming, and relatively few were produced. As a result, there is less variety in cast than in wrought iron.

What we call "tin" is not really pure tin at all, but thin sheets of iron coated with molten tin in order to prevent rust and to achieve an attractive surface appearance. The metal tin, while malleable and extremely rust-resistant, is of such low tensile strength that it is rarely used by itself.

Tinware first appeared in the seventeenth century. The iron sheets on which tin was poured had to be hammered thin and flat by a man called a "beater." This was slow and difficult work, and the product was, consequently, too expensive to be of much practical use. In the following century, though, giant rolling machines were developed that produced thin and inexpensive sheets of iron ideally suited to tinning.

There are two distinct types of tinware—plain and japanned. With plain, the iron is protected and made attractive by the silvery-gray tin coating alone, though this may be decorated in various ways—by piercing, engraving, or repoussé. Japanned tin is coated with a thick layer of a black tarlike substance known as asphaltum varnish. Once dry, it can be painted with floral and geometric devices. Such tin is known as toleware (from the French *tôle*, meaning, logically enough, "sheet iron"). Though both varieties are collected, tole is preferred, followed by engraved or pierced tin. Plain ware (which constitutes the great majority of all tinware) brings up the rear.

Tinware is really a product of the 1800s, for it was during that century that it really came into its own, gaining much of the market formerly dominated by pewter, brass, and copper. Large factories in Europe and North America turned out vast quantities of tin utensils that were sold so inexpensively that all could afford them. Lighter than pottery and glass, tin was used primarily for household items such as plates, cups, storage containers, pots, and pails.

Because tin objects had to be soldered together from individual pieces, they were rather weakly constructed. It is in part because of this fragility that, despite its former abundance, much tin, particularly early and uncommon objects such as portable showers and writing paraphernalia, has vanished. This loss is also due to the fact that tin was so inexpensive. It was just too cheap to mend. If a piece was damaged it was discarded. Fortunately for the collector, though, a great deal of European and American

tin still exists, and it offers a wide field of interesting artifacts.

Much European tin, in fact, has not yet come to the attention of collectors. The Austrians made baking tins in the shape of grotesque animals and fabulous creatures for the preparation of *gugel hupf*, a cake baked only for special occasions such as holidays and weddings. French tinsmiths produced tole lamps and lanterns and, during the Empire period, vases and jardinieres made and painted in the classical manner. The Spanish are best known for their tin pole lamps *(faroles)*, which are large, many-sided lighting devices fitted with colored glass reflectors. Though not yet as important as copper, brass, and iron, European tin is coming into its own as a relatively inexpensive yet interesting antique.

English tin, too, is important to collectors today. The English were the first to industrialize their tin industry, and during the past century they produced a bewildering variety of tin objects, both plain and japanned. There are tablewares such as tureens, tea and coffee sets, salt cellars and pepper boxes, egg cups and drinking cups, jelly molds, and various cooking vessels. Many of these items imitate in style the Sterling and Sheffield silver of the same period. There are lighting devices ranging from simple candlesticks and whale-oil lamps to elaborately painted tin chandeliers and sconces. There are spice boxes of all kinds, many painted to simulate bamboo or wood graining, a technique typical of the Victorian period. There are even large and unusual pieces such as bathtubs and portable shower-baths.

European copper, brass, and iron offer a wealth of choices to the collector. In no other area of the world does one find the quantity and variety of metalware available in England and on the Continent.

In the British Isles copper and brass have always been

highly prized. Sophisticated mining techniques were introduced by a group of German miners in 1566. In the 1680s, James II granted the Braziers Company (the brass-makers' and coppermakers' guild) a monopoly on copper- and brasswork, as well as the right to examine and test all wrought and hammered brass and copper made in London.

Among the most prized of all old English copperwork are weathervanes. Erected on public and private buildings as wind directionals and status symbols, the vanes are made of pure copper, hammered to shape over wooden patterns and then gilded or painted. Often they are more than 6 feet (1.8 m) tall. For many years strict regulations dictated the sort of weathervane a building might have. Churches bore a crowing cock or the figure of a saint. Public buildings and castles used a banneret, often with the owner's initials cut into it. Guildhalls or public markets often flew an appropriate occupational device, such as the large fish commonly seen over fish markets. The largest English weathervane extant is the early-nineteenth-century 11-foot (3.4-m) grasshopper that stands atop London's Royal Exchange. In Europe and particularly

in America, weathervanes are now regarded as folk art, and collectors eagerly seek them out on house- and barntop.

There is much more collectible English copper. Cast cooking pots are early and relatively uncommon, but there are many examples of hammered and riveted ones, as well as other household utensils, including fish kettles, the oblong copper pots some 2 feet (61 cm) long that were used for baking or steaming large fish. From this vessel originates the expression "a pretty kettle of fish." Nor should one forget larger items, such as the tinned wash boilers once so essential to the Saturday night bath and now popularly used as planters.

Other sought-after collectibles are the copper fire-insurance plates, or firemarks, which, in the days before municipal fire companies, marked the homes of those who had paid their premiums and were thus entitled to aid from the insurance company's engines. These marks are often decorated with a phoenix or a rising sun and may bear the company name and policy number. They are extremely desirable but have been reproduced in recent years, so buyer beware!

Among English kitchen copper, jelly and pudding molds are preeminent. These are found in many different shapes, including flowers, animals, human figures, and geometrics. The Duke of Wellington alone had more than five hundred molds in various floral and figural forms, all bearing the cipher DWL (Duke of Wellington, London). Many other wealthy families had similarly marked molds, and these command a higher price in the antiques market than the unmarked variety.

Collectible English brass includes such things as candlesticks and trivets, but more unusual items are found as well. For the sportsman there are nineteenth-century pear-shaped powder flasks, which were stamped out of

sheet brass and bear embossed hunting or sporting scenes. Horse lovers are attracted to horse brasses of the same period. These are cut or cast disks about 3 inches (7.6 cm) in diameter that were (and in some areas still are) hung on the forehead, chest, and sides of a horse during festivals or other special occasions. They are primarily decorative, though some see them as a reflection of the ancient talismans used to protect animals from the evil eye. Horse brasses are found in hundreds of different patterns, some purely abstract, others, such as the Tudor rose and the Jacobite acorn, with distinct political overtones. They are attractive and widely collected, but one should be wary of modern examples in thin, stamped metal.

Mention should also be made of English brass door knockers and fireplace equipment. The former, particularly the ornate knockers of the Georgian period, which show traces of Chippendale influence, are frequently miniature works of art. Brass fireplace equipment became popular in the eighteenth century and has remained so. Some of the most interesting pieces were designed in the late nineteenth and early twentieth centuries by artisans influenced by the Arts and Crafts movement and may show Art Nouveau or later Art Deco characteristics. These are perhaps not strictly antiques, but they are in constant demand and show well the ability of the brassworker to adapt to changing styles.

Continental copper and brass was more highly decorated than that of England. The French, in the eighteenth century, made elaborate copper ewers decorated with engraving and repoussé, as well as quaint religious effigies in beaten copper decorated with champlevé enamels. The French also made excellent brass. They developed the brass chandelier, and their candlesticks, unlike most brasswork, reflected definite stylistic trends, following in form the current examples in silver.

Though they made much copper, Dutch craftsmen excelled in brass. Much of their work was hand hammered and decorated with pierced designs and repoussé. Particularly well known to collectors are eighteenth- and nineteenth-century Dutch brass tobacco canisters and matchboxes. These were often engraved with pictures of ships or political leaders, or, at a later date, scenes of the Dutch countryside. Similar boxes are found in copper, usually with engraved brass lids. (It should be noted that the two metals were often combined not only in Holland but in the metalwork of many other countries as well.) The Dutch also employed shiny brass milk pans and dairy utensils. Their two-handled milk pans, skimmers, and water cisterns are all much sought after.

Germany has a long and illustrious history of copper and brass manufacture. The copper mines at Mansfeld, which have operated for more than seven hundred years, are the oldest in Europe; and German craftsmen taught the art of copper smelting to other nations.

In copper, the usual items are found; more unusual work is reserved for brass. German brass is elaborate and massive, with much floral embellishment. Among the outstanding forms are tankards and large ewers or aquamaniles, pitchers in the form of animals real or grotesque. Engraved locks and lock plates were also of high quality, and these provide a highly specialized area of collecting.

Copper and brass also were widely used in southern Europe. Brass utensils were found in the ruins of Pompeii, and the metal was utilized by Renaissance craftsmen. Eighteenth- and nineteenth-century Italian copper was also of good quality. Typical of this ware are the large copper dishes known as *conca* made in the province of Lazio and decorated with simple floral and abstract motifs. In northern Italy, smiths made buckets and footwarmers ornamented with chiselwork.

Spain and Portugal, which for the most part still shun central heating, not surprisingly have produced some of the finest brass and copper warming pans and braziers. The warming pans, which have long handles and were used to heat cold beds, are decorated with abstract floral and geometric designs of Near Eastern origin. Somewhat similar ornamentation is found on the copper and brass braziers in which charcoal was burned to provide a portable heat source. Examples of both forms, dating to the nineteenth century or earlier, may be found in the shops and flea markets of Madrid and Lisbon. It should be noted, however, that modern examples are also being made.

Though ironware has been made for centuries throughout Europe, it was Spain that saw the finest flowering of this art. Spanish iron ore was famous in ancient times, and Greek colonists were mining it as early as the sixth century B.C. By the time of the Moorish invasion, in 711 A.D., Spanish smiths had developed a distinct style.

The first Spanish ironware was not the usual kettle but the sword, a double-edged weapon so effective that the Roman conquerors adopted it for themselves. Nor did the quality of Spanish metal deteriorate in later years. During the sixteenth and seventeenth centuries, the steel blades made in Toledo from highly refined iron were sold throughout the western world, and most military men used these weapons when they could obtain them.

Characteristically, Spanish iron is wrought, not cast, and it has long been used to decorate the outside of houses and in the making of furniture. *Rejas,* or iron screens, and window grills are among the oldest and most picturesque examples of Spanish ironwork. Diagonal iron braces and large, decorative iron bosses and nailheads distinguish Spanish furniture.

Spanish weathervanes are of wrought iron rather than copper, and are crowned by graceful crosses tipped with spirals and stylized floral patterns. Antique Spanish weathervanes are beginning to attract the attention of collectors and promise to be a new area for exploration.

Spanish iron door knockers are also highly collectible. The earliest, from the sixteenth century, are simple flat-backed plates with a movable ring or vertical hammer joined to them. Later and more interesting examples take the form of birds, lizards, or, more typically, a human hand gripping a ball. Other interesting iron pieces are candelabra (some as much as 6 feet [1.8 m] tall), and cooking utensils, which include spoons, spatulas, and forks with incised geometric decoration, as well as small hooked racks on which these implements are hung. The racks often display, in miniature, the same fine curled ironwork seen on grills and gates.

But, of course, Spain had no monopoly on ironwork. Much fine ware was made elsewhere. In France, where the sign of the smiths' guild was a group of horse, mule, donkey, and ox shoes crowned by a figure of St. Eligius, patron saint of the craft, ironmasters crafted remarkably complex locks for trunks and chests. They also made weathervanes and hearth and kitchen implements, including ornate hooks used to suspend cooking pots above the fire. Even today the traditional French expression signaling the beginning of a party is "to hang up the hook."

German founders cast firebacks, flat pieces of iron with raised designs, often biblical or heraldic in nature, used to protect the brick at the back of a fireplace, as well as elaborate cooking and heating stoves, grave markers, and small human and animal figures to be offered at the altar of St. Leonard, patron of prisoners and animals.

Scandinavia has had a long history of ironwork, with Sweden perhaps the best-known source. Iron candlesticks have been a specialty with the Swedish since the Middle Ages. They also made, during the eighteenth and nine-

teenth centuries, cut-iron grave markers that consisted of the name and date of death of the deceased, as well as a depiction of his home, a church, or some religious symbol such as an angel or a cross.

There is also much English iron available, particularly heating and cooking equipment. Great chimney cranes (right-angle brackets that fit into the fireplace to support cooking pots) are found, as are mechanical roasting jacks used to turn meat on the fire, and long-handled, shovellike implements known as slices or peels, used to remove baked goods from the oven. The English also made many different types of smoothing irons: box irons with a hollow space for a hot brick, flatirons, and the heavy, or "sad," irons used by tailors. All are now collectible.

Metalworking is a long-established craft in the Middle East. Over the past few hundred years, Turkish artisans have produced much engraved and inlaid copper, some of which, like the ewers and basins known respectively as *ibrik* and *tisht*, is also decorated with applied enamels. There are also trays with embossed human and animal figures. These generally date from the late nineteenth century and are easily obtained. Turkey is also known for its brass braziers and collapsible lanterns with pierced decoration.

From Syria come finely engraved brass writing boxes covered with arabesques and geometric devices, as well as ewers with iron handles ornamented with applied grotesque masks and shellwork. Syrian brass also includes bowls and trays inlaid and engraved with hunting scenes and floral devices.

Throughout the Near East various iron and copper objects are also found, from weapons to cooking utensils inlaid with thin strips of gold and silver, a technique known as damascene work (named for its association with the city of Damascus).

185

In Asia, too, there is a long history of base-metal use. Dark red copper vessels have been found in pre-Christian Han tombs, and Chinese craftsmen have produced many attractive objects in copper, brass, and iron, ranging from household utensils to weapons and horse trappings.

Perhaps the most unusual of such wares are iron flower pictures. Beginning in the seventeenth century, Chinese artisans attempted to capture in metal the delicate beauty of calligraphic paintings. Using wrought iron, the workers copied and framed popular paintings. The earlier and better examples, dating to the eighteenth and nineteenth centuries, are hand wrought, riveted together, and mounted in wooden frames. Later pictures (some of which are still made today) are machine stamped from thin metal and lack the artistic quality of their predecessors.

The Chinese have also produced much brass, both utilitarian and decorative. Finely finished small brass fireboxes or braziers with pierced decoration may be found, as well as brass and copper tinderboxes. The latter are tube-shaped receptacles for flint and steel, decorated with engraved scenes. Most available braziers and tinderboxes date to the 1800s, but collectors can find later brass. From about 1890 until well into this century, the Chinese manufactured many ashtrays, pillboxes, cigarette boxes, trays, and vases of brass inlaid with enamel, glass, or semiprecious stones. These were often marked "China" and were widely distributed throughout the world. They are now being collected.

Japan also had its workers in brass and copper, but there all nonprecious metal, even bronze, took second place to iron. As early as the twelfth century Japanese smiths were famous for their iron weapons and armor, and few will dispute the preeminence of the Japanese sword blade. Japanese swords are often signed by the maker, and they are of great interest to sophisticated collectors.

More than sword blades are collected. The *tsuba*, or sword guard, and the *kotana*, the handle of a small eating knife usually affixed to the scabbard of the *wakizashi*, are both highly decorated and therefore highly collectible. *Tsuba* are usually of iron, circular or slightly elliptical, and about 3 or 4 inches (7.6–10 cm) across. They are decorated with piercing, engraving, gold and silver inlay, and even enamel. *Tsuba* are miniature versions of the finest products a Japanese metalworker could make. *Kotana* are less elaborate, usually of bronze ornamented with applied human or animal figures cast or wrought in gold, silver, or iron.

Other Japanese ironware was closely associated with local customs. The ritual tea ceremony required several vessels, among them a finely molded and engraved cast- or wrought-iron teapot. Such pieces were always very simple, in keeping with the austerity of the ceremony. But there were also more elaborate Japanese wares, such as iron vases inlaid with gold or silver that were made for both export and domestic use during the late nineteenth century.

Japanese craftsmen also manufactured many brass items. One of their more unusual contributions was the pistol-action flintlock tinderbox, designed so that pulling the trigger would explode a small quantity of gunpowder, which in turn would ignite the tinder. The cases for these tinderboxes were usually decorated with piercing and inlay in precious metals.

Despite the importance of Chinese and Japanese brass, the major source of collectible Oriental brassware and copper is India. The people of the Indian subcontinent preferred copper for their cooking vessels and produced many unique variations. These were often of a regional nature. For example, Kashmir in the north was famous for brown copper coffeepots inlaid with black lacquer, while

copper gilt toilet boxes with ornate locks were made only in the Punjab. From other areas came such items as *surahi*, the tall containers for Ganges river water, and many types of hammered copper trays and dishes.

Indian brass is found in even greater variety than Indian copper. Brass has for many centuries been used in the casting of small religious figures. During the 1800s, Nepalese artisans modeled figural groups, primarily hunting or sporting scenes, for sale to the European market.

Brass utensils are also common. From Moradabad, in northern India, come tin-lined plates, water jars, and sugar pots; and from Hyderabad, farther south, there are ewers, bowls, and basins. The decorative techniques vary. Engraving is practiced in Moradabad, for example, while in Hyderabad decorative designs are inlaid in copper and highly polished. So distinct are these regional differences that experienced collectors can often recognize the origin of a piece of Indian brass by its design or decoration alone—a good thing, since such pieces are rarely marked or otherwise identified.

Most Indian brass made prior to the late nineteenth century was cast or beaten to shape; the many lathe-turned or spun pieces seen are usually of this century. Many of them, particularly inlaid boxes, candlesticks, and vases, were made for export and are marked "India" or some variant of that mark.

Among the more popular and obtainable Indian brass objects of a somewhat earlier date are teapots, bells (both the small, handled temple bells with finials in the shape of gods or demons, and bullock bells), and betel-nut cutters in human or animal shapes. And, of course, there are the brass, or sometimes copper, hookahs, or water pipes. These exotic creations are not really very old by antiquarians' standards, since smoking was not introduced into India until the late seventeenth century. But they were made in great quantities, and few tourists can resist the temptation to take one home. One should, however, keep in mind the fact that hookahs are still made, and most seen in Indian shops are only a few years old.

Brass and copper were also employed in other areas of Asia. Tibet, for example, is known for its brass tea mortars and drinking bowls and its wrought-copper urns and samovars. The samovars, ornamented with brass medallions and animal-head finials, are particularly attractive. Such items are relatively scarce compared with Indian and Chinese metal.

Compared with that of other parts of the world, the history of North American metalwork is short indeed. Native Americans did not use the base metals, and early settlers' efforts to fabricate them were frustrated by English laws designed to make it difficult for local industries to get started.

There were iron smelters in Massachusetts and Virginia during the seventeenth century, but until 1750 most ironware used in North America was imported. Once political and economic freedom were obtained, American iron masters began to produce a great variety of objects. Most of them, however, were patterned after their European antecedents. From New England came wrought tools and hinges not unlike those of Birmingham; from Pennsylvania, cast stoves and firebacks that could be taken for the German examples their makers had grown up with. It was some years before American and Canadian ironwork charted its own course. Until then, it was distinguished from its European counterparts primarily by its greater volume and simpler decoration. Since few iron pieces are marked, this similarity has presented problems for North American collectors who, in seeking the products of their forebears, must be able to distinguish them from imports.

191

Peruvian copper mask representing
the deity Ai-Apec, Middle Mohica style,
3rd century A.D. Copper was known
and worked at an early date in South America.
This ritual mask was hammered to
form over a wooden mold and embellished
with applied work and inlay.
The punched holes and eyelets indicate
that the mask was intended to be
worn or attached to a figure of some sort.

Similar problems beset the tin industry, which had to rely on imported metal until the middle of the nineteenth century. Nevertheless, there were tinsmiths in New England during the 1700s, and soon after the beginning of the next century the industry began to expand. Small tin shops sprang up throughout New England and New York, and their products were carried across the country by peddlers.

The discovery of tin deposits in the West spurred the industry, and industrialization led to the creation of large factories that were turning out vast quantities of plain tin as well as enameled tinware (tin plate covered with a protective coat of porcelainlike material) by the end of the nineteenth century. Toleware and plain tin decorated with pierced and punched work, which are highly prized by collectors today, were all but abandoned by manufacturers after 1850, and good examples are now rare and expensive. Enameled ware, on the other hand, was produced well into the twentieth century, and its bright and cheerful colors have made it extremely popular with collectors.

There was little American-made copper or brass prior to about 1850. Foreign competition and problems in developing local mines made life very difficult for domestic manufacturers. True, there is a rare marked warming pan by the eighteenth-century Boston coppersmith Charles Hunneman, and there are some brass andirons by the illustrious Paul Revere, but for the most part the ware that was produced looks so much like its European counterpart that collectors are frequently in a quandary as to attribution of specific pieces.

Around the middle of the last century, though, the combination of new discoveries of ore, increased capital, and the use of metal-spinning devices led to a rapid expansion of the American copper and brass industries. Spun-brass pots and kettles, many of them marked by their manufacturers, poured out of Connecticut shops. They are considered highly desirable by collectors today. Most copperware was made in small shops, though copper weathervanes were produced in sizable factories. These vanes took many forms, from the rather common horse to such exotica as trains and sidewheel steamers. Good examples often command very high prices on the antiques market.

The metal trades took a somewhat different course in South America. Pre-Columbian societies were familiar with copper, and copper masks have been found in Peru. The Mixtecs and Casa Grandes of Mexico also worked the metal, as did several tribes in Costa Rica.

Following colonization, European iron and tin were introduced, and many kitchen utensils, grates, spurs, and stirrups of iron wrought in the Spanish-Moorish tradition may be found throughout South America. Tinware has also been produced for many years. There are eighteenth-century church candlesticks and altar sets in the metal that were made by native craftsmen after Philip II forbade them to work in their traditional silver.

South American metalware—primarily bowls, trays, and covered dishes—is distinguished from that of Europe not only by its heavier, cruder quality, but also by the frequent use of decorative motifs clearly related to traditional native mythology. Such devices as the winged dragon of the Aztecs and the solar and lunar signs associated with the Incas may be found interwoven with floral and geometric designs of Spanish or Portuguese origin.

Copper, brass, iron, and tin are as vital to us today as they were a century ago; and the increasing interest in antiques in these mediums will go far to preserve a heritage of craftsmanship important to an understanding of eighteenth- and nineteenth-century life.

9
Woodenware and Basketry

Preceding pp.: Chinese woven bamboo and painted
lacquer box, late Ming dynasty (early 17th
century). The carefully done design in gold leaf is
typical of fine early Chinese lacquerwork.
Above: American wooden utility pail, 19th century.
The delicate hand-done decoration is
similar to the work found on painted American tin.

There are few societies indeed that have not created and made abundant use of wooden and basketry objects. The variety of collectible items in this category is extensive enough to allow for much specialization. Some may collect Asian baskets, others North American butter molds or European decorated boxes. Still others may choose broader categories such as kitchenware or old wooden tools. In most cases, the collector, whatever his or her field, will find extensive assortments of relatively inexpensive and attractive objects.

The more primitive wooden objects are those that are entirely handmade, either by carving or by carving and charring. It has been many years since wooden bowls, for example, were shaped by hand in Europe; but even today, African and South American natives burn and hew such vessels into shape. The technique involves cutting a wooden block the approximate size of the object to be formed, then hollowing it by burning out the center bit by bit. Once this is done, the exterior is shaped by carving. Such woodenware always bears the telltale chip marks of the cutting tools used.

In more sophisticated societies woodenware is turned on lathes, either hand- or water-powered. An object formed on such a lathe has many concentric circles on its surface, indicating where the cutting blade of the lathe shaped the exterior of the turned object.

The more desirable examples of woodenware are generally those that are unusual in form and decoration. Primitive peoples and the rural populations of more advanced nations are likely to produce the most lavish decoration. This may be of several different kinds. Pieces may be deeply carved with various pictorial or geometric designs, they may be painted in one or more colors, or they may be inlaid with wood of a contrasting color.

Though far less variety of form exists, basketry objects also may be attractive and appealing to the collector. Unusual items, such as fish traps and animal cages, may be found, but most basketry is simply that—large or small containers of many shapes and purposes. Weaving may be quite simple, as in the splint crosshatch baskets of North America, or extremely complex, as in the coiled and braided baskets of Asia. Materials vary from the bamboo and rattan favored in China and Japan to the grass and rough vines employed in some areas of Africa. In all cases the collector looks for good form and interesting decoration.

Collectors are drawn to old wooden and basketry items for several reasons: nostalgia, the attractiveness and decorative value of certain examples, general small size, and reasonable prices. But these are only a small part of the story. The real key to the growing appeal of these antiques is the fact that the best examples are folk art in the truest sense. Many of the finest wooden objects were made to be given as gifts, and they were made with great care and skill by people with a long tradition of craftsmanship.

Regrettably, however, few of these craftsmen are now known to us, even though most of them worked in the eighteenth and nineteenth centuries. This relative lack of age and obscurity of origin are characteristic of wooden and basketry items and sharply distinguish them from most other antiques. Though dated eighteenth- and even seventeenth-century examples may be found, most woodenware and basketry collected today is no more than 150 years old. Moreover, though many pieces bear names and initials, they can rarely be associated with a known craftsman. Most carvers and basket weavers remain anonymous. There are exceptions, to be sure, such as the famous Norwegian woodcarver Jacob Klukstad (c. 1715–1773), whose workshop in Gudbrandsdal became famous throughout Scandinavia. Klukstad introduced a carved

1

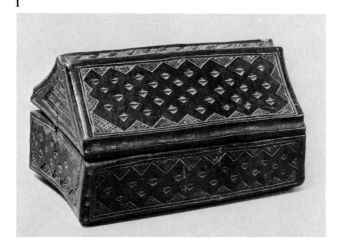

2

3

198

acanthus-branch motif as decoration for furniture and small utensils and established a style that endured for a century. He is, however, almost unique. Few others in his craft have attained fame.

That the best-known carver should have come from Norway is perhaps understandable, for Scandinavia has produced some of the finest decorative woodenware. Surrounded by trees and with limited resources in other raw materials, the people of northern Europe turned early to wood as a means of supplying their household needs. In Sweden and Finland nearly all eighteenth- and nineteenth-century utensils were made of wood decorated by carving or burning. As in most areas, geometric and floral motifs were most common, but pictorial elements are also found. Bold representations of dragons, eagles, lions, and horses are worked into such objects as spoons, hanging boxes, and farm tools.

Carving was the earliest and most important form of decoration in these areas, but painting also played an important part, especially in Norway, where the technique of *rosemaling* (rose painting) was developed in the 1750s. *Rosemaling* was, essentially, the use of stylized flower and leaf motifs, particularly the rose, to ornament everything from woodenware and furniture to wall paneling. The style, based on medieval illuminated manuscripts, was popular among country people until the end of the nineteenth century. Sophisticated collectors have been interested in *rosemaling* for some years, and chairs, cupboards, and smaller items so decorated are much sought after in Europe.

The Scandinavians were also skilled at making staved objects—barrels, casks, and drinking vessels composed of curved pieces of wood bound together with metal or wooden hoops. They were so fond, in fact, of their staved tankards that their contemporary silver and pewter drink-

4

ing vessels were often modeled on wooden examples.

A bit farther south, the Germans excelled in various forms of woodenwork. The medieval custom of giving small boxes or caskets as love tokens lingered long here, and as late as 1900 peasant craftsmen were making so-called chip boxes or brides' boxes—covered oval containers 3 to 16 inches (7.6–30.6 cm) long and up to 6 inches (15.2 cm) high. These pieces were made of thin strips of wood, steamed or soaked until flexible, then bent around and pegged or nailed into an oval wooden base. The boxes were sometimes decorated with incised designs, but the majority were painted in bright colors. The earliest (seventeenth-century) decoration consisted of a marbleized background on which appeared swirls and spirals in a contrasting color and, sometimes, abstract floral decoration. By the early 1700s the pieces were being ornamented with full-length portraits of soldiers, lovely ladies, and haughty gentlemen. This type of subject matter continued to be used for as long as the boxes remained popular, though originality and quality of design deteriorated toward the end of the last century. The area around Berchtesgaden was the center of manufacture for these boxes. The cheerful colors and interesting subject matter of brides' boxes have endeared them to collectors, both in Europe and in North America, where they are often taken for similar local examples made by Germanic immigrants.

The Germans did outstanding carving as well as painting. The handles of their mangle boards (flat boards used for pressing clothes in the days before irons) were cut in the shape of fabulous animals such as griffins and unicorns, and the designs carved into spoon handles and the bowls of salt cellars were sometimes inlaid with bits of colored wax. (The technique of inlaying wood with colored wax, known as wax intarsia, was also used in furniture decoration.)

England also has a strong woodenware tradition. Finely carved knitting needles and stay busks (stiffeners inserted into the bodices of women's dresses) were regularly given by men as gifts to their sweethearts. Appropriately, these objects were covered with a network of geometric devices into which were worked hearts and flowers, dates, and the initials of the lovers. The earliest known of these tokens is a knitting-needle case dated 1686.

Very popular among collectors are English gingerbread molds—flat, rectangular pieces of wood with shallow carving. These were used to decorate gingerbread, which was impressed with them prior to baking. The designs were both attractive and topical. As an example of the latter, there are early-nineteenth-century molds that bear a representation of the Biddenden Maids, a pair of Siamese twins who captured the imagination of the country folk.

Butter pats and molds, which were used to shape and decorate fresh butter, are also found. These are very attractive, and some have historical interest. At times a standard design was used to identify all butter marketed from a given region—for example, the rose motif found on molds from the Preston area.

English country craftsmen also delighted in straw marquetry, the practice of ornamenting such things as boxes and mirror frames with bleached and split straw, which was glued to cut-away areas on the surface of a darker wooden object in order to provide a contrasting pattern. Straw marquetry originated in France or Spain in the seventeenth century but was most widely practiced in the Dunstable area of England, where it became a major cottage industry, particularly during the nineteenth century.

The most interesting French woodenware is found in Brittany, where wooden spoons were so lavishly carved that their owners proudly wore them as waistcoat ornaments. These spoons were made both of thin, flexible

1

2

3

wood and of thicker, more durable material, and they might be carved or inlaid with colored wax or tiny bits of mother-of-pearl. Brittany spoons are frequently dated (as befits objects of such high quality), and known examples range all the way from 1675 to 1870. They are still available though becoming increasingly difficult to find.

Other areas of France had their specialties as well. Alsace was known for its turned spinning wheels and decorated cake molds, while the shepherds of the Pyrenees made everything from carved animal collars to milking chairs, walking sticks, and necklaces for their loved ones. The enforced loneliness of the shepherd's life seems to have encouraged creative carving, for some of the finest of all European woodenware comes from the high sheep country.

This is certainly true in Italy, where shepherds' crooks and staffs were often finely formed and decorated with the mystic signs of the planets. The rural craftsmen here also made delicately engraved spoons, forks, and ladles, as well as milking stools and yokes.

Like English examples, Italian butter molds often bear designs specific to a particular area. Examples are the edelweiss motif associated with Valle d'Aosta and the burning heart of Ticino. Another interesting form of Italian woodenware is the *grolla*, a huge gobletlike cup that was used only on special, festive occasions. The body of the *grolla* was turned on a lathe, then body and lid were carved in relief with a wide variety of biblical and mythological figures.

Unlike most of western Europe, Portugal and Spain are nations where folk crafts still flourish on a wide scale, and chief among these crafts is the working of wood. The Alentejo area of Portugal is famous for its elaborate flax swingles (the upper portion of the flail, a two-part tool for separating grain from chaff) and ox yokes. The yokes are

4

large, often 6 feet (1.8 m) across, covered with stylized carved symbols, and richly painted with floral, geometric, and mystic designs. Another Portuguese specialty is cork work. Boxes and salt cellars are lightly carved and painted with floral motifs and scenes of village streets or phases of the bullfight.

A substantial amount of fine Spanish woodenware is also available. From Zamora come large ladles with handles in the form of a church belfry, from León there are the finest castanets made in Europe, and from the southern hills there are shepherds' crooks with tips carved in the shape of human or animal figures, and spinning distaffs inlaid with bone and decorated with gilded nails. Mortars, spoons, and baking molds are also common, many of them, like the distaffs, bearing the unmistakable mark of Moorish decorative techniques.

Though it is collected to some extent, European basketry is not yet truly appreciated, and this is an area in which the discerning collector can acquire a representative grouping for a relatively modest sum. One should keep in mind, though, that because of its fragile nature, there is little basketry that is more than a few decades old. Look for form and decoration rather than antiquity. Since the art of basketmaking is largely dying out, any attractive example is collectible, regardless of age.

Good basketry sources are Spain, where the marketplaces are still filled with woven fruit and vegetable containers, and France, where until recently every village had its own basketmaker. Look for the deep, handled grape-gathering baskets, shallow straw containers, and elaborately woven, often heart-shaped, cheese forms. Less commonly found in France today are animal muzzles of splint or rush and the once-common willow cradles. Not very long ago, the latter were made in great quantity in the Haute-Marne for shipment throughout the nation.

French basketmakers have used many materials besides the favored willow—there are crab and fish traps made of myrtle, woven straw beehives, mulberry-vine storage containers, and tiny grass thimble covers.

Basketry was also practiced in Austria, where firewood carriers were woven of bark and twigs, and in Germany, where natural-colored willow baskets were embellished with the addition of dyed materials, including (in Bavaria) strips of stained leather. Baskets may be found in every country of Europe, and the collector may pursue his or her interest with assurance that the field is relatively open.

North American basketry and woodenware are an interesting mixture of European and native influences. Canadian and American Indians were making baskets and carving bowls long before the arrival of the first white men. Lacking iron tools, they shaped their wooden objects by burning and gouging with stone adzes. Some of the things they made, such as the log canoes, totem poles, and statues found in the Northwest, were quite large and required many hours of hard work.

Caucasian settlers brought with them the skills of their native lands, and much nineteenth-century American woodenware clearly reflects European antecedents. In Pennsylvania, German-born settlers carved and painted chests and brides' boxes little different from those of Germany and central Europe. In Wisconsin and Minnesota, Scandinavian immigrants decorated their boxes and cupboards with *rosemaling* exactly as they had done in their homelands. And in the Southwest, coarse pine was used to make furniture and utensils that, in their employment of iron strapwork and Gothic carving, clearly indicated their debt to Spanish examples.

As in all useful crafts, however, the Canadian and American examples differed from their foreign antecedents in being much plainer and more utilitarian. Form

followed function, for in the face of a wilderness function was all-important.

Basketry too was an Indian craft, and Indian basketry, whether it is the coiled straw work of the southwestern United States or the dainty sweet-grass baskets of the Canadian Maritime Provinces, continues to be a most popular area of New World collecting. The European settlers also made many baskets, but the introduction in the late nineteenth century of factory-made basketry largely put an end to individual white basketmakers. The Indians, on the other hand, have persevered. Indian basketmakers still work in many parts of North America. Most of their output, naturally, goes to collectors and tourists.

Nor has woodenware entirely vanished in the face of technological advances. The artisans of the late-nineteenth-century Arts and Crafts movement loved wood and shaped it in many ways, often combining it with copper and ceramic insets. Even the renowned Tiffany and Company employed this humble medium, inlaying it with glass and metal to make such things as boxes, desk sets, and candle stands. Tiffany wood is possibly the most expensive of all woodenware today.

In South America, also, the native peoples worked in wood and basketry materials before they were exposed to European influences. Most of their early creations have been destroyed, but traces of them may be seen in the wares produced by present-day Indian craftsmen. The Seris people of northwestern Mexico, for example, produce excellent woven baskets, known as *coritas*, that are strikingly similar in design and decoration to those made by the Indians of the American Southwest. In other nations, such as Colombia and Chile, there are native groups that carve and decorate their wooden eating utensils with motifs similar to those found on pre-Columbian pottery and stonework—a clear linkage to the past. South Amer-

ican basketry and woodenware are now attracting deserved attention not only from collectors but also from the governments of the lands in which they originate, which recognize them as an important national heritage.

Since woodcarving has always been one of the most important Polynesian arts, it is hardly surprising that some of the most interesting wooden artifacts come from the Pacific islands. Wood was far more important than clay as a material for household utensils in this area, and great care was lavished on the making and decoration of bowls and similar objects. In Samoa and the Solomon Islands craftsmen carved bowls in the form of turtles or birds, while in other areas the exteriors of wooden vessels were carefully carved in complex openwork designs featuring curvilinear, tendrillike motifs. The surfaces of such pieces were highly polished by being rubbed with plants containing silicic acid.

Many Polynesian fighting clubs and dance staffs (long sticks used in religious dances) are also decorated, frequently with magical symbols intended to bring good fortune to the owner. Club heads and handles are covered with rectilinear and geometric designs set into panels. These may be incised with a sharp instrument, or they may be burnt in, a technique also employed with lime containers made from native gourds.

Chinese and Japanese artisans have, of course, made extensive use of woodenware and basketry. Pungent camphor wood and dark teak were used by nineteenth-century Chinese craftsmen to make a variety of small chests, boxes, and trays, many of which were sold to Europeans. These pieces were often inlaid with porcelain plaques, mother-of-pearl, or even pewter. Similar chests and boxes are made today, but these are often of unseasoned wood, which cracks when exposed to modern heating.

Other interesting Chinese wooden objects are boxwood combs, heavily gilded and painted lanterns, and small teak stands for displaying pottery and jade. One might also mention the wood and bamboo cricket traps and cages, which were made to accommodate those most interesting insects. (Crickets, valued for their "singing," were kept as pets by the Chinese.) Though most are much later, some cricket cages date to the mid-nineteenth century.

Rattan is the favorite Chinese basketry material, and many different baskets and boxes have been made from it. Probably the most popular of these among western collectors is the round rattan sewing basket decorated with Chinese coins and colored glass beads. Most of these date to the late nineteenth or early twentieth centuries. Though still available, they are becoming harder to find.

The Japanese, in keeping with their more Spartan way of life, have used less woodenware than the Chinese. They have always favored bamboo for basketry and have also used it for making many different household articles. Anyone who attends the Japanese tea ceremony will remember well the delicate bamboo water dippers, or *hishaku*, some of which are as much as two hundred years old. Other common eighteenth- and nineteenth-century bamboo objects are brush holders, needle cases, and the armrests popular with painters and scholars.

The most valuable of all Japanese woodenware are the tiny netsuke, togglelike objects intended to hold the *inro*, or medicine pouch, to the belt. Netsuke are carved from wood (or ivory or horn) into many fanciful shapes, and the best are works of art and priced accordingly.

One can state with little hesitation that woodenware and basketry present one of the most exciting of all present-day collecting fields. A vast quantity of material is still available, much of it very interesting, most of it still inexpensive. A word to the wise collector should be sufficient!

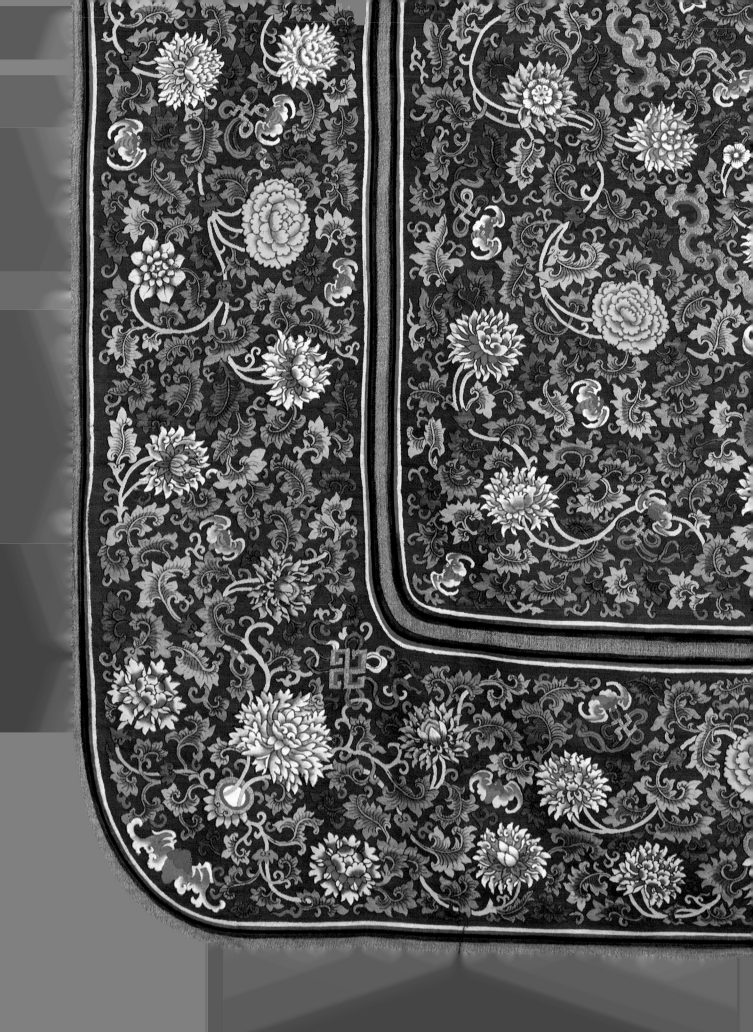

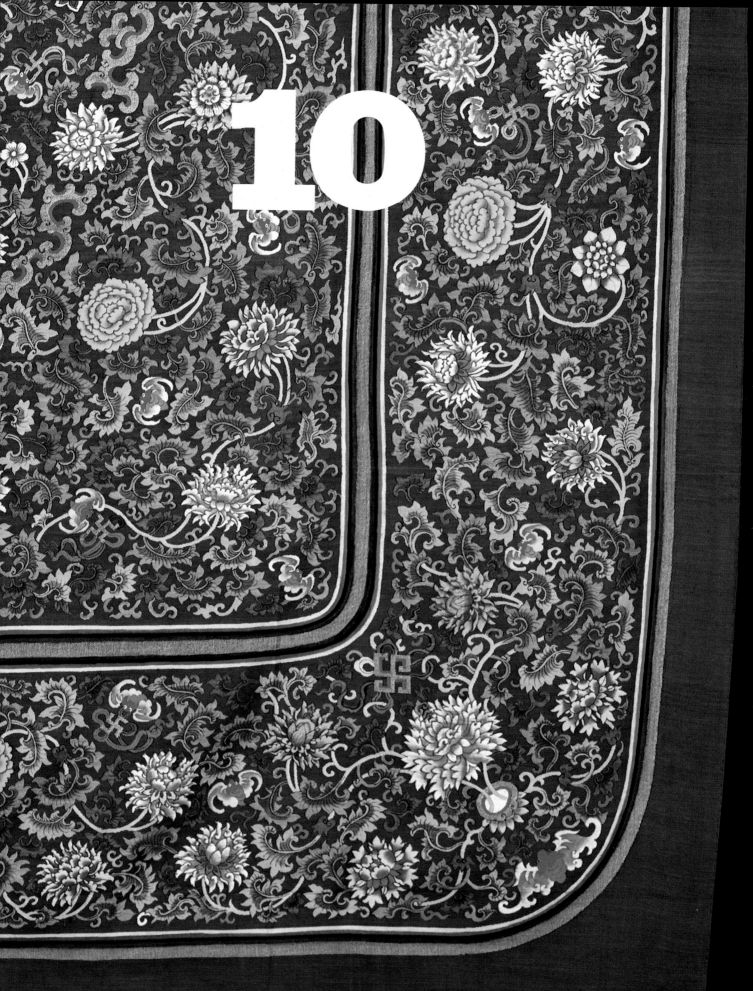

10
Textiles

Preceding pp.: Chinese silk tapestry bedcover,
Ching dynasty, c. 1750. This cover is elaborately
woven in a floral pattern and embellished with
painted detail. Above: English sampler on cotton,
1856. This sampler bears the name of its
creator, Mary Jones. Large building, birds, and
trees mark this as a desirable pictorial sampler.

No area of the world has produced such a wide variety of fabrics as Europe. Not only do the earlier and traditional handmade textiles such as embroidered and woven fabrics appear here, but it was also in Europe that the first steps were taken in industrializing textile manufacture.

Hand-woven tapestries, generally pictorial or floral in composition, appeared first in ancient Egypt, but their greatest development took place in Continental Europe. Their style and subject matter conformed to the changes in taste evident from the Gothic period through the Neoclassic. Though related to furniture and wall decoration, tapestries were viewed more as fine art. They were produced by highly skilled craftsmen who followed rigid rules of design and composition. The subject matter of European tapestries nearly always consists of one of the following traditional subjects: religion, history, allegory, mythology, or romance.

It is generally agreed that the finest work was done in France from the fourteenth to the eighteenth centuries. So highly regarded was the field of textiles in the 1700s that well-known academic artists like François Boucher (1703–1776) created patterns for tapestries. Many of Boucher's designs were woven at Beauvais and Gobelin, the two famous Parisian tapestry manufactories. A strong rival to France was Belgium, where the Brussels factories produced some outstanding work, particularly during the sixteenth century. The renowned *Acts of the Apostles*, designed by Raphael, was woven in Brussels in 1519.

Tapestries have always been popular among antiquarians, and few good early examples are obtainable. However, smaller and less well-known pieces from the eighteenth and nineteenth centuries do come on the market and can sometimes be purchased for reasonable sums. These should, though, be distinguished from machine-woven, factory-made late Victorian tapestries.

Very different in origin from the professionally made tapestries are samplers. At a very early date, young women and girls in Europe and the British Isles began to make small, embroidered needlework pictures designed to display their skill at various stitches and, in some cases, their knowledge of the alphabet and the numbers from one to ten. The earliest written reference to a sampler occurs in the account book of Elizabeth of York, a noblewoman, who noted, on July 10, 1502, an expenditure for "an elne of lynnyn cloth for a sampler for the Queene." A few dated sixteenth-century samplers are known, but most are from a later period.

Existent examples and pictorial evidence indicate that the first samplers were made in southern Europe, probably in Italy and Spain, and that from there the skill spread northward. One thing is clear—many pieces are remarkably similar in their composition. They may consist of nothing more than numbers and letters, or they may include pictorial elements such as houses, people, and animals. The earliest samplers were long and narrow, since looms of the time could weave only narrow strips. By the 1700s samplers had grown quite large; then, in the early nineteenth century, they became more or less standardized at about 14 by 16 inches (35.6 × 40.6 cm). Most samplers have distinct pictorial elements, but there is little doubt that many were made from patterns. In fact, the first sampler pattern book was published by an Englishman, Peter Quentel, in 1527.

Samplers are widely collected in Europe and North America. Those most sought after are the ones that have pleasing pictorial designs and those that can be identified by name and locality. Condition is also important, for many samplers are badly faded or worn.

There is much more European embroidery, including ornamental needlework pictures and crewel work—

214

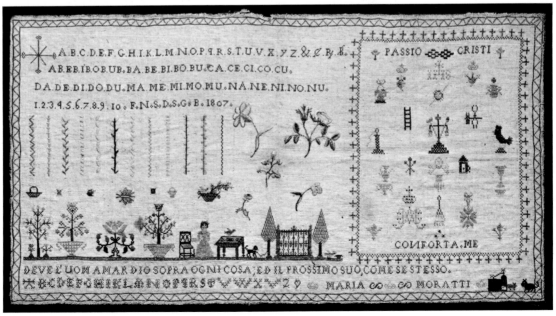

spreading, ropelike designs, created with brightly colored yarns and used to make pillows or to decorate overstuffed furniture.

As industrialization spread across Europe, much handwork was supplanted by factory products. Needlework was no exception. In 1760, Philip Oberkampf, a German cloth printer, founded a factory near Versailles, France, for the mechanical printing of cotton and linen. His designs, which were typically pictorial in nature and done in a single, soft tone on a neutral background, were greeted with such enthusiasm by the nobility that in 1783 Louis XVI made Oberkampf's establishment a royal manufactory. Within a few years fabric printing was sweeping through western Europe. It was cheaper and faster than hand printing (particularly after the development of rolling presses) and made decorated textiles available for the first time to the great majority of the population. Though they are, to some extent, a product of the machine age, printed textiles are especially popular with collectors who seek out small items such as the handkerchiefs printed to commemorate important people or events. These printed cotton handkerchiefs must have been made and exported in some quantity, for they (or design elements cut from them) frequently show up in eighteenth- and early-nineteenth-century American quilts.

Textile manufacture in North America has, to a great extent, paralleled that of Europe. Since textile items could be made by nearly every woman, and since, unlike many other crafts, the raw materials for needlework were as available in the New World as the Old, American and Canadian women practiced their arts from the first days of settlement.

The earliest achievements seem to have been samplers. There is an American sampler from the 1640s made by Loara Standish, daughter of the well-known Captain Myles Standish. The Standish sampler is not only very well executed, it also contains the first of the many pious aphorisms found on seventeeth- to nineteenth-century pieces:

> Lord guide my hand that I may do thy will
> And fill my heart with such convenient skill
> As will conduce to Virtue void of shame
> And I will give the glory to thy Name.

There are quite a few other seventeenth-century American samplers, and women in the United States practiced the art until late in the nineteenth century. Few post-1850 samplers are of much interest, however—most appear to have been made from commercial patterns.

Sampler collecting is very popular in the United States. Some people are quite satisfied to collect any example, domestic or foreign; but those who seek only American pieces face certain problems. Unless they bear a recognizable local place name, American samplers are practically indistinguishable from imported English and Irish examples. Even German pieces may be found, and these are very similar to those made by the Pennsylvania Dutch.

Another very popular form of New World textile art is the woven coverlet. English, Scottish, and Continental European weavers brought simple looms to the Colonies, and with these they made bed and table coverings of heavy woven cloth. Coverlets are typically of wool and cotton, though some early wool-and-linen and all-wool examples are known. The most common types are overshot coverlets and summer-winter coverlets. The former are woven so that the woolen threads skip over the cotton ones for several inches at a time, leaving a distinct woolen ridge—hence the term "overshot." Summer-winter coverlets are reversible, with darkly dyed wool predominating on one side and undyed cotton on the others. The contrast between the dark and light sides led to the use of the name "summer-winter coverlet."

Overshot and summer-winter coverlets are always made in geometric patterns, for the looms that produced them could make nothing else. They are generally in two or at the most three colors, with blue and white, red and white, and red and green being the most common combinations. These bed coverings were made as early as the mid-eighteenth century, though few pieces from the 1700s are known—the earliest dated example is 1811. They are still being made, primarily by rural women in the southeastern United States, who sell them to tourists and collectors.

In the early 1820s another type of coverlet appeared. A Frenchman named Joseph Jacquard had developed a device that, when attached to larger looms, made it possible to weave coverlets with curvilinear as well as geometric patterns. With the Jacquard looms weavers could produce all sorts of floral and pictorial bed coverings. These were made in Europe, of course, but it was in the United States and Canada that the art was perfected.

From 1821 (the year of the first dated American Jacquard) to 1918, when Albert Graf of Ontario, the last North American weaver, closed his shop, thousands of Jacquard makers produced tens of thousands of bed coverings. The patterns found among these are extremely varied. There are representations of the Great Seal of the United States; of George Washington, General Lafayette, and other historical figures; of trains, ships, and houses; and of many different kinds of birds and animals. By the 1870s, the introduction of steam-powered looms and aniline dyes led to more varied colors. Originally limited to one or two hues, as the geometric coverlets had been, Jacquard fabrics now appeared in four or more colors.

Woven coverlets are very popular with American collectors, who regard them almost as historic documents. Generally the earlier Jacquards are favored, for these tend to be more inventive in design. The late Victorian examples follow standard patterns and are made from inferior materials.

By far the most important contribution of American women to the history of textiles is the quilt. Sometime during the mid-eighteenth century, two types of bedspreads or coverings began to appear in North America. These were the appliqué quilt and the pieced, or patchwork, quilt. They are basically similar in structure: each consists of a front, which bears the design; interior batting (usually of cotton) for warmth; and a plain or printed backing. The three parts are sewn or quilted together in layers, a technique known to the Chinese hundreds of years ago.

The appliqué quilt is made by cutting out various design elements such as flowers, hearts, and animal forms, and sewing these to a piece of solid cloth with simple buttonhole stitches. In the earliest appliqué quilts, such as one made in Virginia in the 1770s, the design elements are usually cut-out portions of a patterned imported chintz or Oriental calico. At a later date scraps of domestically produced cotton fabric were employed.

Patchwork quilts are constructed in a different manner. Pieces of scrap material are cut into geometric forms—squares, stars, triangles, and the like—and sewn together to form the front of the quilt. (Curved pieces of material are rarely used because these are difficult to sew together.) During the late Victorian period (1870–1910), the crazy quilt, a variation of the patchwork quilt, appeared. Unlike prior pieced quilts, crazy quilts were made of scraps of velvet, satin, or silk and were stitched together with embroidery floss in fancy chain stitching. Since they were quite fragile, most crazy quilts were used as table coverings or furniture throws rather than bed covers.

In both appliqué and pieced quilts, one of the most important aspects in determining quality is the quilting itself, that is, the stitchery that binds the three elements of the quilt together. In most cases the quilting is very plain, perhaps no more than straight lines running back and forth across the piece. In more desirable bed coverings, though, the quilting may be quite elaborate, with floral patterns and figural devices worked into the fabric.

Quilting was a practical way to make warm, serviceable bed coverings from old scrap cloth, but it was also much more than that. Often, quiltmaking became a social event. Women from miles around might gather for a quilting bee, and, in a single day, while gossiping and singing, they might put together one or more complete quilts. One of the favorite quilting-bee projects was the friendship quilt, on which each worker would inscribe her name or a verse. Another was the album quilt, which was composed of many different squares, each made by an individual and all put together at a bee.

Quilts were traditionally part of the trousseau a young woman might prepare for her "hope chest." Some idea of the importance attached to this tradition may be gained from the following verse, embroidered on a nineteenth-century quilt:

> *At your quilting, maids don't dally.*
> *A maid who is quiltless at twenty-one,*
> *Never shall greet her bridal sun.*

For the past decade quilts have been among the most popular American antiques, and the rage for collecting them has now spread to Europe. It is not uncommon for dealers to take as many as a hundred quilts to France or Germany, where they can be sold for even higher prices than they bring in their country of origin.

221

Among the most exquisite of all textiles are those that have been produced in the various countries of Asia. As in so many of the useful arts, China is preeminent here. As early as the sixteenth century, Chinese embroidery was being exported to Europe in large quantities. Most of this work was done in small shops in Peking or Canton, and favored decorations included portraits and realistically stitched pictures of birds, flowers, and insects.

Large frames covered with satin were arranged on movable turntables, and the design to be worked was lightly sketched in pencil on the base fabric. Then, using tiny tufts of silk floss dyed in various colors and needles so fine that they could be handled only by someone with soft, uncallused fingers, the embroiderer would stitch the design as though he or she were painting a picture, overlapping stitches to create contrasting shades, and changing colors at will. Among the best known of embroideries so created are the large squares used in making the gowns worn by Mandarin families in the eighteenth and nine-

teenth centuries. Embroidery of lesser quality was made by the yard (particularly in the province of Hunan) for use in pillow cases, drapes, and bedspreads. Embroidery was also used to decorate handbags, cosmetic bags, and fans, many of which were intended as wedding presents. Embroidered objects of this sort are among the most available and most popular of Chinese textile collectibles.

Chinese tapestry work, known as *kó ssu*, is a form of weaving employing fine silk threads. A background is first woven in thread of the smallest diameter. Then this background is opened up with tiny shuttles, and a decorative design in somewhat heavier thread is woven into the spaces. *Kó ssu* pictures are usually no more than 1 by 3 feet (30.5 × 90.4 cm) in size, and they are relatively uncommon outside China. Chinese craftsmen also made larger tapestries of heavier material. These were often embellished with gold thread.

The Chinese are, of course, also well known for their brocades of woven and embossed silk, and the few available early court costumes in this material are highly prized by collectors. Actually, though, some of the most interesting examples of this work were done in Japan. The Japanese learned how to make brocade from the Chinese, but they elaborated on the art. The best known of their innovations is patchwork brocade, which consists of many different squares varying in design and color scheme. This fabric was supposedly developed at the behest of a noble who decided to have a gown made from all the pieces of brocade he had available at the moment. If the early examples were, indeed, sewn together from different squares, it was not long before the Japanese learned how to weave a single piece of material that achieved the same effect. Early Japanese brocades were very stiff, as may be seen from thirteenth-century paintings in which the nobles appear to be wearing garments of painted cardboard. At a later date, however, Japanese craftsmen mastered the fine, soft patchwork brocade of which their kimonos were made in the 1700s and 1800s.

Some of the loveliest and most folk-oriented material found in the Orient comes from Malaya and Indonesia. Hundreds of years ago the Malayans mastered the art of batiking. In this process the craftsman creates a pattern on a piece of white cloth, usually cotton or silk, by marking out a design in dye-repellent clay or wax. Then the whole piece of cloth is dipped in a dye bath. When the wax or clay is removed, the undyed portions stand out in pattern against the dyed areas. The earliest patterns seem to have been in blue and white, but later techniques involving multiple dippings allowed for more complex designs and many different colors.

The Indonesians also were masters of block printing or stamping. This is another very old technique and, basically, a rather simple one. A motif is carved into a block of wood, which is then dipped in dye and applied to a piece of material of a contrasting color. Most Indonesian block printing was done on relatively small pieces of cloth, though in Japan whole bolts of cotton were printed in this way by teams of workers.

Embroidery is regarded as a fine art in India, where it has been practiced since at least the fourth century B.C. It is, in fact, quite possible that the art spread from here to the rest of Asia. Though all Indian embroidery is well thought of, highest praise is reserved for that of Kashmir, where workers specialize in elaborate designs and unusual color combinations. Kashmiri shawls have long been regarded as a luxury in the West.

India is also well known for its chintz—cotton cloth printed or painted in many hues. The *palampore,* a chintz bedcover, was very popular in England during the 1700s. In fact, Indian chintz was imported into the British Isles in such quantity at that time that restrictive laws were passed to protect the domestic textile industry.

A form of stamping or block printing was also practiced in Polynesia, particularly in the Hawaiian Islands. However, since they had not developed cotton or flax cultivation, the Polynesians used bark cloth, or tapa cloth. The outer bark of a tree was scraped off and the inner bark soaked and beaten until it was soft. This was then pressed out in long strips on a flat board and compressed until a paperlike substance was obtained. Tapa cloth was decorated with hand-painted or block-printed geometric motifs, and it was used to make clothing and masks.

Only a relatively few textiles from relatively few countries are actively collected today, and because of the fragile nature of the material, most of what is available is of fairly recent origin. Nevertheless, the importance of textiles to all peoples and the obvious care that has been devoted to their manufacture and decoration make them an important area of antiques.

11
Toys

Preceding pp.: Set of English cast-lead
miniature soldiers by W. Britains Ltd., early 20th
century. Britains is the largest modern
producer of military miniatures. Above: French
bisque-headed doll by Jumeau of Paris,
late 19th century. Jumeau was one of the most
famous of all doll manufacturers.

No society, even the most primitive, has existed without toys for its children. Hobby-horses were known to the Greeks at the time of Socrates, and rag dolls have been found in ancient tombs in such widely scattered localities as Egypt, China, and Peru. The origins of such objects are lost in time, but there is no doubt that toys were once much more significant than they are today. Dollmaking, for example, seems to have developed from the manufacture of religious figures, and even as late as the nineteenth century some societies perceived the doll to be much more than a plaything. In the West Indies and parts of Africa voodoo dolls have been used in ritual magic, and until quite recently Chinese children did not play with dolls, for human figures were regarded as too sacred for such use. Those Chinese dolls that do exist are, for the most part, twentieth-century items intended for export.

In many societies, toys were viewed as instructional devices to be used in the training of young children. Books, for example, seldom only told a story. More often, they were intended to teach a religious lesson or to enforce basic social precepts. Thus a writer in the *Boston Weekly Newsletter* of February 26, 1727, admonished his readers that children's play should serve a practical purpose, for "it is likewise intended that their very Recreations shall be made profitable to them, either to their health or understanding or rather to both: that Virtue and Godliness shall be encouraged among them and Vice discountenanced by all means possible. . . ."

A child's toys might also serve to protect him or her from harm. The rattle, that simplest of all amusements, was at one time a talisman. Coral-and-silver rattles made in Europe and North America in the eighteenth and nineteenth centuries were thought to be capable of forecasting and even of warding off disease. These small objects consisted of a tooth-shaped piece of coral set in silver with bells attached. Good health was anticipated as long as the coral remained its natural deep red, but if it became paler, it signaled impending illness. In Japan, the figure of Shoki, the legendary devil chaser, served a similar purpose. This awesome figure, dressed in elaborate, flowing robes, was believed to be able to banish evil and sickness. From the sixteenth century on, nearly every Japanese boy has owned such a figure.

But, in the past as today, most toys were intended solely as playthings, and it is this connection with childhood and its amusements that has made toy collecting one of the fastest-growing of all hobbies. Collectors throughout Europe and the United States are scouring antique shops and country sales for these small mementos of the past. Though toys have been made for centuries in virtually every part of the world, most collectors find that their acquisitions come from one of three areas—Europe, North America, or Japan. There are, of course, playthings from other regions, but in number and variety they cannot compare with the items made in the shops and factories of the major toy-producing nations.

Most collectible playthings date from the period 1850 to 1940. Foremost of these are dolls. Thousands of people collect them, and doll-collectors' clubs number in the hundreds worldwide. Many of these organizations are located in Japan, where dolls have been designed, dressed, and collected for hundreds of years, and where dolls are often as important to adults as they are to children.

Collectible Japanese dolls are of several types. Least expensive yet extremely interesting are the *kokeshi*, small, turned wooden figures that are shaped something like bowling pins and have loosely jointed heads that jiggle when the figure is moved. *Kokeshi* developed during the Edo period (1614–1864), and the first ones were simply cheap wooden toys for poor children. In time, however, they became more elaborate, with brightly painted faces and bodies. They have been sold in Japan for more than a century, and many examples are available in the West.

Even more important are the Japanese festival dolls *(hina ningȳo)* and the so-called cherry dolls *(sakura ningȳo)*. The former are sets of figures that are displayed on shelves during the Girls' and Boys' Festivals, seasonal celebrations that are important events in every Japanese family. The small dolls have carefully enameled faces, ornate hairdos, and richly brocaded costumes in styles dating to the sixteenth century. For the Girls' Festival on March 3rd, there is a grouping that includes the Emperor and Empress and various court attendants. Dolls for the Boys' Festival of May 5th are dressed as warriors and folk heroes and are accompanied by miniature weapons and the model of a war horse. Festival dolls are still handed down from generation to generation in Japanese families, and their display gives parents an opportunity to instruct children

in the traditions of family and country.

Cherry dolls are almost exclusively adult toys. Lavishly dressed in silk and satin and made up to resemble figures from the Japanese Kabuki theater, they are displayed in the home, almost as works of art.

Festival and cherry dolls are considered highly collectible not only in Japan, but also in the West, to which they have been exported since the late 1800s. An older, well-dressed doll by a well-known maker or with an interesting family history may bring a very substantial price, though most specimens can be obtained for much less.

European dolls are found in much greater variety than those of Japan and, with the exception of manikins or fashion dolls, they are intended primarily as playthings rather than display items.

As in most areas of the world, the earliest dolls in Europe were made of wood. Jointed wooden dolls were known in England during the fourteenth century, and un-

til well into the 1800s the least expensive and hence the most widely available dolls were of wood. In Germany and Austria a cottage industry developed for the manufacture of these figures. Toymakers in such towns as Nuremberg and Oberammergau turned out large quantities of flat-faced, slope-shouldered figures with pegged-on arms and legs. These were given a traditional paint job (shiny black hair, red shoes, red cheeks) by country women working for the equivalent of a halfpenny per dozen. These dolls are generally referred to as Dutch dolls (probably because they were shipped abroad through Holland), though a similar English form is known, called the penny wooden in reference to its original price. Quite a few examples of eighteenth- and nineteenth-century Dutch dolls and penny woodens may be found today.

Many collectors favor the finer, bisque-headed dolls that were made, primarily in Germany and France, during the mid- and late nineteenth century. The best-known man-

ufacturers of these creations are the French firms of Jumeau and Bru. Pierre Jumeau won his first award for doll design at the Paris Exposition of 1847, only five years after he had set up shop. In the next half-century his company turned out thousands of delicate-featured, finely dressed dolls. These were of two distinct types: the childlike *bébés* and the smaller, fastidiously clothed *poupées.* A formidable competitor, Léon Bru, entered the field in 1867, and for the rest of the century, these two manufacturers largely dominated dollmaking. Today, marked Jumeaus and Brus sell for high prices.

There were also European dolls made from other materials. Wax-headed dolls were made in Italy, France, and England, with the finest examples produced by London's Montanarit and Marsh families from 1850 to 1900. Paper dolls were also popular. In the 1760s the French created *pantins*, little, flat pasteboard figures whose movable limbs jerked when a string was pulled. These jumping jacks were forbidden by law in the bizarre belief that women might become pregnant by manipulating them. At a later period (1890–1940) the English firm of Raphael Tuck was known for its punch-out paper dolls.

Until well into the last century most dolls in America were imported from Europe. The local manufacturers were either enterprising copyists like Joel Ellis of Vermont, who, in the 1860s, patented a jointed doll that was really only an improved penny wooden, or folk carvers like Wilhelm Schimmel of Pennsylvania (1817–1890), who wandered the countryside carving toys in exchange for room, board, and a glass of schnapps. Ellis dolls are considered rare and sell for quite a bit of money. Schimmel pieces are considered folk art and sell for much more.

By the middle of the nineteenth century, however, American dollmakers had begun to come into their own. Ludwig Greiner of Philadelphia took out the first American patent on a papier-mâché doll head, Albert Schoenhut opened the 1900s with his Humpty Dumpty Circus, a collection of jointed wooden figures and animals, and in 1915 John Gruelle made the first Raggedy Ann doll. What Americans might have lacked in style and sophistication they made up in ingenuity. They created the first rubber doll, the first celluloid doll, the first movie-star dolls—a veritable parade of playthings, and today's collectibles.

Closely associated with dolls are dollhouses, or "baby houses," as they were called until the 1850s. The earliest known dollhouses are Dutch and German examples dating to the sixteenth and seventeenth centuries, but the great majority of those available to collectors are from the second half of the last century. By this time mass production had made it possible to sell houses and their furnishings at prices that most people could afford. Earlier dollhouses had been handcrafted, one-of-a-kind items. Some, indeed, were exact replicas of their little owners' homes.

The furniture used in Victorian dollhouses is as much in demand as the structures themselves. Duplicating in style and form the actual furnishings of the period, such pieces were even made of woods appropriate to the time—oak, rosewood, and walnut, for example.

Related to the dollhouse are individual room or shop settings, such as the well-known Nuremberg kitchens. Each of these three-sided representations of nineteenth-century kitchens contained a fireplace and miniature heating implements as well as detailed copies of all the cooking and baking utensils of the period. German, English, and American manufacturers also produced a variety of shop constructions reproducing as accurately as possible tinsmiths', bakers', or blacksmiths' shops. Since many of the tiny accessories to these structures were lost, complete shops are prized by collectors.

Toy dishes, particularly tea sets, may be found in everything from wood to Britannia metal, but the most highly prized examples are in earthenware or china. Since the sixteenth century European kilns have made such children's toys, often duplicating in miniature the popular ware of the period. Thus it is possible to find Dutch Delft, Spanish majolica, or English Staffordshire, all designed to suit the needs of youngsters. The Chinese even made export porcelain for children. Among the popular and relatively inexpensive children's pottery of the late 1800s are Wedgwood plates decorated with pictures of characters from children's literature, such as Jack and Jill and the Sunbonnet Babies.

If little girls had dolls, then it was only fair that boys have an equivalent, and this was the toy soldier or military miniature. The earliest of these tiny, detailed figures were painted wooden infantrymen made in Egypt around 2000 B.C. The first metal figures appeared much later. Young Louis XIII of France was given an army of ceramic, lead, and silver soldiers in the early 1600s, and by the end of the century manufacturers began to make the toys available to the general public.

The first shops to sell toy soldiers were in Strasbourg, Germany, and their wares consisted of flat tin figures (hence the term "tin soldiers"). Tin proved too fragile and was soon replaced by an alloy of tin and lead. From the early eighteenth century until the 1850s, hand-painted flat tin soldiers were the most popular. Most of these were made in Nuremberg, Germany, where they were sold wholesale by the pound.

In 1789 a Parisian named Lucotte made the first three-dimensional molded lead soldier, and by 1828 three French factories were producing these. Lead soldiers (which are really made of an alloy of lead and antimony) gradually replaced the flat tin figures, for they were more realistic. The best-known late-nineteenth-century manufacturer was Mignot of France, and the twentieth century has been dominated by the products of the Britains Company of London, which made lead soldiers until the 1950s.

Other famous twentieth-century makers of military miniatures were Alexandre Ballada, who devised the idea of casting components of miniatures separately, so that they could be used interchangeably; Stadden, who made extra-large and exotic figures such as officers of the Indian army; and Otto Gottstein, a well-known creator of dioramas incorporating as many as 18,000 figures.

Collecting tin and lead soldiers is an extremely popular hobby, and there are many collectors' clubs. Even the twentieth-century figures are regarded as highly collectible in Europe and North America.

It was in the second half of the nineteenth century that toy factories arose in western Europe and North America. Some of these factories limited their output to dolls and toy soldiers, but most of the big shops made other things as well, chiefly tin and iron toys.

Lightweight tin toys, which were usually such things as carts, animals, and representations of early trains or ships, were very popular with nineteenth-century children. The earliest of these toys were made in the late eighteenth century of sections of metal that were hand-cut, soldered together, and then painted. Such toys were relatively expensive, and few examples have survived. By the 1830s, however, manufacture had become more sophisticated. Stamping machines were used to cut out parts more rapidly, and chromolithography, like that used in printing, was utilized to print rather than hand-paint bodies. Because of these new techniques, the volume of toys made increased sharply, while unit prices declined sufficiently that all could afford to own a tin toy.

The most attractive and sophisticated tin toys were pro-

duced in the United States and Germany. In 1856, George W. Brown and Company of Forestville, Connecticut, began manufacturing tin toys, many of which were activated by wind-up, clockwork motors. In 1868, Edward R. Ives, a Connecticut neighbor, entered the field, and his factory, in Bridgeport, became one of the world's largest and longest-lasting toy companies, remaining active until 1930. Brown and Ives toys are regarded as the *crème de la crème* by sophisticated collectors in both America and Europe (where they were often copied in the days before international patent laws), and it is not unusual for an early marked piece to cost as much as a modern automobile.

The tin toys made by these and other firms were truly products of the new industrial age. Not only were they made on assembly lines in factories, but, in form and type, they mirrored the advances of technology. Early examples copied the animals, horse-drawn conveyances, and sailing ships of the early nineteenth century, but as the world changed so did toys. The development of the train, the steamboat, and the bicycle were reflected in the manufacture of highly accurate copies in miniature. As the twentieth century dawned, toy automobiles, zeppelins, and, finally, airplanes appeared.

During the 1870–1920 period (considered the "golden age" by collectors), these tin toys were made in great quantity. Factories in America and Germany produced thousands of pieces a day. Many of these have long been lost, of course, but large numbers have survived. Nevertheless, collector demand is so great that there are not nearly enough good-quality toys to go around. Prices are high and competition fierce. As a consequence, some collectors have turned to later examples, such as those produced in the United States during the 1930s by the Marx Toy Company. A new area that is just starting to be explored is the post-World War II clockwork tin toys of Japan and Germany. From 1945 through the 1950s, extremely high-quality animated toys were made in the western-occupied sections of both countries. Examples of these are still readily available and relatively inexpensive. They offer the collector an opportunity to gather a selection of high-quality toys at a reasonable cost.

Cast-iron toys were developed later than their tin counterparts, primarily because they were more expensive and time-consuming to produce—most toys were cast in several pieces and then bolted together. Some English and American cast-iron banks date to the 1860s, but the industry did not become fully established until the 1880s. Thereafter, a bewildering variety of objects appeared,

234

some of which were still being made as late as 1940. Best known and most appreciated by modern collectors are cast-iron vehicles and mechanical banks. The former include elaborate, horse-drawn fire engines as well as later vehicles such as airplanes and World War I-vintage military tanks. All were hand-painted, for lithography could not be employed on three-dimensional figures.

Mechanical, or "animated," and nonmovable, or "still," banks are very popular with collectors. Animated banks are those that perform some action when a coin is deposited. A good example is the so-called Tammany Bank, a seated figure with an extended hand. When a coin is placed in its hand the figure promptly puts it in its pocket, an allusion to the greed of the Tammany political machine that dominated New York City during much of the late nineteenth and early twentieth centuries. Banks often carried a political message. Another example is the English still bank that portrays, in an unflattering manner, President Paul Kruger of the Transvaal (now a part of South Africa), a bitter enemy of the British at the end of the last century.

Cast-iron vehicles and mechanical banks are so eagerly sought after at present that original, authentic examples cannot begin to meet collector demand. Unfortunately, this situation has led to extensive reproduction and outright faking. Using either original molds or molds made from original figures, unscrupulous persons have cast figures, painted them and then artificially aged the paint, and palmed them off as originals. Collectors must proceed with caution in this field.

Fortunately, however, there are areas of toy collecting in which supply at least equals, if it does not exceed, demand. One of these is board games. Traditional games such as backgammon and checkers were played in the eighteenth century, but it was not until the Victorian era produced a middle class with sufficient leisure time to devote to games that the modern board games were developed. These are usually boxed games with movable counters activated by a spinner or by cards chosen by the participants. The basic principles of play are seldom complex, which in part accounts for the great popularity of the games as family entertainments.

Perhaps the earliest American board game was the "Mansion of Happiness," issued in 1843 by Ives, the tin-toy manufacturer. In the following year the same company came out with the game with the longest name—"The Game of Pope and Pagan, or the Missionary Campaign, or the Siege of the Stronghold of Satan by the Christian Army." In this game, the goal was to advance along a path from earth to heaven, with participants' movements determined by spinning a numbered dial. In keeping with nineteenth-century mores, these games were moralistic and educational. Similar games were soon produced in France and in England, where "Constantinople" and "Willie's Walk to See Grand Ma" were popular late-1800s creations of A. N. Myers of London.

There were literally thousands of nineteenth- and early-twentieth-century board games, many of them known today only through advertising material. Since they were usually made of paper and cardboard, most of these games have been destroyed or are found in a mutilated state. It is a challenge to discover a good example, but the collector is rewarded by lovely, lithographed box covers and a fascinating insight into Victorian customs and ideals. And, best of all, board games are cheap.

There are many other kinds of toys: marbles, tops, sleds, skates, hobby-horses, and so on. All have their devoted collectors and always will, for no area of antique collecting can touch the heart in the way that these playthings of our ancestors can.

Index

References to illustrations in italic numbers

Photo Credits

America Hurrah, New York—228 (top), 231 (btm).

Asian Art Museum of San Francisco, The Avery Brundage Collection—19, 110-111, 194-195.

Austrian Press and Information Service, New York—44 (btm right).

The Brooklyn Museum—30-31, 102; The Frank L. Babbott Fund: 54 (top); Gift of Miss Susan D. Bliss: 42 (top); Gift of Mrs. J. Amory Haskell: 50 (top); Gift of Mrs. Ernest Vietor: 52; The Caroline and Alfred Zoebisch Fund: 106.

Canadian Consulate General, New York—51.

Chrysler Museum at Norfolk—Gift of Walter P. Chrysler, Jr.: 130-131, 134; Joan Foy. French Collection: 139 (top); Gift of Dr. Eugen Grabscheid: 139 (btm).

Bob Cihi / Antiques Magazine—170-171.

Copyright The Frick Collection, New York—41 (left), 150-151; Childs Frick Bequest: 35.

Hillwood, Washington, D.C.—143, 163 (left).

Landrigan & Stair, New York—43, 45.

Lisa Little / The Metropolitan Museum of Art, New York, The Michael C. Rockefeller Memorial Collection of Primitive Art—119, 154 (btm), 182 (top), 198 (right).

The Metropolitan Museum of Art, New York—95 (left), 98 (top left), 118 (top left), 208 (top right); Bequest of Benjamin Altman: 156 (top right); Gift of Mrs. S. P. Avery: 97; Gift of H. L. Bache Foundation: 71; Gift of the Members of the Committee of the Bertha King Benkard Memorial Fund: 189; Bequest of Dorothy Graham Bennett: 108 (left); Bequest of Kate Read Blacque: 118 (right); Gift of Mrs. J. Insley Blair in memory of J. Insley Blair: 103, 104, 105; Bequest of Susan Dwight Bliss: 112, 117 (top), 172; Gift of George Blumenthal: 123, 125, 127 (btm), 165 (btm right); Gift of John C. Cattus: 128; The Cloisters Collection, Purchase: 202 (top); The Cloisters Collection, Rogers Fund: 179 (right); Gift of Russell Cowles: 39 (top); Gift of Nathan Cummings: 192; The Theodore M. Davis Collection, Bequest of Theodore M. Davis: 75; Gift of Mrs. Robert W. de Forest: 185, 203, 204 (right); Gift of Mr. and Mrs. Robert W. de Forest: 81; Harris Brisbane Dick Fund: 57, 80, 160 (top); Gift of The Dillon Fund: 23 (top); Gift of Joseph M. Drexel: 76 (top left); Gift of Mrs. Lucy W. Drexel: 68, 176 (btm), 177; Gift of Mr. Lewis Einstein: 85; Fletcher Fund: 36, 137 (right), 201 (top), 214 (left); The Michael Friedsam Collection: 8; Friends of the American Wing Fund: 47; Gift of Edgar William and Bernice Chrysler Garbisch: 10-11; Gift of Hugh J. Grant: 191, 208 (left); Gift of Mrs. Charles W. Green in memory of Dr. Charles Green: 148; Purchase, The Lucille and Robert H. Gries Charity Fund: 158; Bequest of Caroline S. Hanway: 61 (left); Gift of Mrs. Edward S. Harkness: 25; Bequest of Mary Stillman Harkness: 12; Gift of H. O. Havemeyer: 147; Bequest of Mrs. H. O. Havemeyer, The H. O. Havemeyer Collection: 199; Gift of Mrs. William Randolph Hearst: 14; Gift of Mrs. Leroy Kent Howe in memory of her husband: 91 (right); Gift of Samuel Isham: 22; Gift of James Jackson Jarves: 141 (left); Gift of Ronald Kane: 169; Robert Lehman Collection: 34; The Morris Loeb Gift Fund: 174 (btm); The Howard Mansfield Collection, Gift of Howard Mansfield: 184 (top); Bequest of Mary Martin: 132; Gift of Mrs. Emily Winthrop Miles: 144 (top left); Gift of Edward C. Moore: 137 (left), 141 (btm right), 152; Gift of J. Pierpont Morgan: 16 (btm), 17, 27, 76 (top right), 162, 179 (left); The Collection of Giovanni P. Morosini, presented by his daughter, Julia: 174 (top); Gift of Giulia Morosini: 181 (btm); Gift of the Rev. A. D. Pell: 76 (btm); Bequest of Alfred Duane Pell: 77; Purchase, The Ella Morris de Peyster Bequest: 28; Bequest of Stephen Whitney Phoenix: 202 (btm); Gift of the Duchesse de Richelieu: 38; The Michael C. Rockefeller Memorial Collection of Primitive Art: 20 (both), 21, 64 (all), 65, 72, 74, 121, 154 (top), 198 (top left & btm left); Rogers Fund: 16 (top), 23, 32, 39 (btm), 44 (left & top right), 46, 58, 87, 90, 92, 95 (right), 96 (both), 98 (top right & btm), 100, 101 (btm), 108 (right), 116 (both), 117 (btm right), 118 (btm left), 160 (btm), 168, 181 (top), 214 (right); Gift of Rosenberg and Stiebel: 202 (middle); Gift of Mrs. Russell Sage: 91, 101 (top), 188 (btm), 204 (left); Seymour Fund: 61 (right); Gift of The Shaw Foundation, Inc.: 82 (left); Gift of Charles Stewart Smith: 156 (left); Gift of Frank Sturgis: 165 (btm left); The Sylmaris Collection, Gift of George Coe Graves: 141 (top right), 145 (btm); Gift of George White Thorne: 159; Gift of Mrs. Katherine Townshend: 165 (top); Gift of Irwin Untermeyer: 66-67, 124; Bequest of Mrs. James H. Wickes through A. C. Brown: 144 (top right); Gift of Alan L. Wolfe: 107; Gift of Mr. and Mrs. Alexis Zalstem-Zalesky: 88.

Museum of the City of New York—226, 228-229 (btm), 231 (top left & top right), 232 (all).

Courtesy Museum of Fine Arts, Boston—78, 79, 82 (right), 115, 138, 163 (right), 182 (btm right), 210-211, 215, 220 (top); Gift of Mrs. Franz Aigner: 220 (btm); M. and M. Karolik Collection: 222; Gift of Mrs. Charles Hamilton Parker: 219 (btm); Textile Special Fund: 219 (top).

The Museum of Modern Art, New York—Greta Daniel Fund: 54 (btm).

The National Gallery of Art, Washington, D.C.—Widener Collection: 40 (both), 41 (right), 122, 127 (top), 156 (btm right), 216 (top).

Nelson Gallery-Atkins Museum, Kansas City, Missouri—Nelson Fund: 63; Gift of the Kenneth A. and Helen F. Spencer Foundation Fund and Mrs. Kenneth A. Spencer: 60, 62.

Philadelphia Museum of Art—142, 221; Given by George Plimpton Adams, Jr.: 201 (btm); Purchased, Baugh Barber Fund: 167 (btm); Given by Mrs. Henry W. Breyer, Sr.: 167 (top); Given by Mrs. George B. Emery: 208 (btm right); The Titus C. Geesey Collection: 50 (btm), 188 (top), 196, 234; Bloomfield Moore Collection: 176 (top); Purchased, Museum Annual Membership Fund: 205; Given by Richard Samson: 184 (btm); Purchased, Special Museum Fund at the A. W. Drake Sale: 178; The Louis E. Stern Collection: 182 (btm left); Given by Alfred Walkenberg: 120; Bequest of Mabel Buck Wheeler: 117 (btm left); Whitman Sampler Collection, Given by Pet Incorporated: 212, 216 (btm).

The Soldier Shop, New York—224-225.

Sotheby Parke Bernet, Inc., New York—42 (btm), 126.

Courtesy the Henry Francis du Pont Winterthur Museum—49, 186, 187, 207.